WALKING in AWARENESS

by Tony Kent

Published by Sidi Muhammad Press
toll free order no. 888-438-7242
Cell Tech Approval no. 121371

This book is dedicated to my friend Joan McGovern.
I love you, Joan.
You have been such an addition to my family
that you have become family;
I am so grateful to you and all that you do,
your help over the past years
has been a big blessing in my life.
Thank you for being there,
and for supporting me in living my dreams.

Contents

Introduction

The purpose of this book is to share with you my attitude and feelings about network marketing as a path of growth and transformation. The book is like a diary, and consists of articles, talks, transcripts of tapes, and just plain musings during the time I was building a large organization, traveling as a trainer and sharing with others my vision. Some of it is repetitious, because it is my story and I have told it many times in many different ways. The material can be read in any order and please feel free to share it in any manner you deem appropriate, especially when you feel it would be helpful to someone.

I was introduced to this opportunity by Kare and Charles Possick, to whom I give thanks. I feel that a large part of the original momentum in my organization can be attributed to the genius that they brought as a team to introducing a new paradigm into the networking opportunity in a manner that allowed me to grow as fast as I did. Without a doubt, I was fortunate to have them as mentors. There are many other people to whom I give thanks, and as I tell my story you will meet them all.

I hope that everyone reading this material will find something of benefit. Even though much of what I write is about Cell Tech, the company with which I fell in love, I believe that anyone in network marketing can use and apply this information because it is more about ***being someone than doing something.***

Before I start I would also like to send love and thanks to Daryl and Marta Kollman, the co-founders of Cell Tech. I love you both and from my heart to yours flows an outpouring of gratitude for creating a place that feels so much like home. God bless you.

And finally, to my guide and teacher Sidi Shaykh Muhammad al-Jamal ar-Rifa`i, I send my heart.

Chapter One

My Story

This is a story with no beginning and no end. I want to share with you a process; a process that totally transformed my life. Many of the things that happened during this process are archetypal, and I am sure you will find your own story within mine. As I traveled the U.S. and Canada sharing what happened in my life with others, so many people came up and said: "That sounds so much like what I am going through."

Let me start the sharing of this process by giving you a brief background. I was born in New York City on August 29th, 1941. I spent the major part of my adult years living in France and working as a fashion photographer. I experienced a very successful career and was fortunate to work for many of the best magazines. During one of my assignments for French Vogue I met and fell deeply in love with a French woman by the name of Nathalie, who was at that time an editor. We subsequently married and had four children together. Meeting and sharing my life with Nathalie felt like a constant showering of magical dust sent down by the Divine, and my life prospered in many ways. In the safety of the love we shared, my heart opened in ways I had not previously known, and the more my heart opened the more I felt I grew as a person. For over 20 years I lived in the blessing of this love until the early 1990's when Nathalie felt the need to experience life on her own. My heart shattered when she left, the pain rendered me totally dysfunctional, and for the next four to five years I lived obsessed with my misfortune, raising four children, and feeling very angry and desperately sorry for myself. One of the therapists I was seeing, a wonderful and loving woman by the name of Ava Brenner, said that one day I would build an alter to commemorate this event in my life, and my thoughts were: "I can't believe I'm paying $80 an hour to hear this."

At that time it felt as if my life was in a shambles. I retold this story many times during my training sessions, and what follows is a transcript off of a tape that I recorded.

I'm going to see if I can empower you with *visualization* which is really what I'm about. The whole thrust of what I have come to share with you is that the future you're going to have tomorrow you actually start creating now. Sometimes very small actions that we take have large powerful consequences in our life. I think in order for you, or for anybody to appreciate what I'm going to share with you in the next couple of days, it's important for you to know my personal story, to understand how I was introduced to Cell Tech, where my life was, and where its gone since then. I've noticed as I travel around the country that my story is an archetypal story. I think a lot of people are going to hear at least part of their story inside my story, and a lot of the illustrations I use are from different people saying the same thing with a different voice. Even though some of the words are almost identical to words that I would choose to use, I hear them mouthed by Daryl Kollman and I hear them mouthed by kids in South Central LA; I've heard them mouthed by Double Diamonds, and algae eaters all over the country. One of the things that I've heard a lot is: algae is a magnet that attracts caring people. Another thing is that an amazing amount of people were at a time in their life where hope was not the most powerful force existing for them at that particular time.

In my case, I was in a deep depression for over four years, and had been through a really traumatic experience. I was single parenting four kids; and if I was good at something at that time of my life it was that I was great at being the victim. It's not a very self empowering place to be, but it was the fact of where I was.

For most of my adult life I had been a fashion photographer and traveled the world, having been very successful in my field. I had a full and enriching life. I lived probably 20-25 years in Paris and outside of Paris. I've been just about everywhere and have photographed some of the most exciting people in the contemporary world. I moved back to America with the hope of exposing my children to my heritage. I had only two of the children at that time. I also had a sense that things in Europe were going to change; that the future was going to be a little bit different than the present, and it didn't look like it was getting a lot brighter. There was a fairly severe economic squeeze, and there was, what I experienced as, a lot of negativity and a lot of depression, especially amongst the young people. I am a big believer in positive thought so I wanted to go back to America so that my kids could experience that freedom. But what happened was that when I got back there my life fell apart.

Everything all unraveled. Imagine there is a big tapestry of the picture of my life, of what I thought it would be like–a successful father, husband, photographer, and a certain lifestyle. It was a pretty secure picture, one that I had formed, obviously, pretty early in my life. That picture fell apart; all the threads of the tapestry were unraveled on the floor, and I was in a lot of fear. I would lie awake at night wondering what I could possibly do.

I had saved some money over the 25-30 years, because being an artist I didn't have anything like social security to fall back on. I went through my life savings very quickly. It was gone in less than two years. It was amazing how I had miscalculated. Sometimes you think $50,000-$100,000 is a lot of money. I'd never actually accumulated that much money because I was always doing things, buying things, spending money, and living well. So even though, in my mind, I thought I had a lot, when it actually came time and I stopped working for six months to a year, or wasn't working at the same rate that I'd been working at, it was amazing how fast the money disappeared. I would lie awake at night and wonder to myself–what could I do? I was very depressed. I was wondering what was going to happen to my children, and what was happening to my family. My wife had really been the social person, and she had a very large family with lots of brothers and sisters. That was my connection out into the universe.

> ## Fear is really just imagined pain.

One thing I've learned since all this fell apart and I was lying there in fear, is that fear is really just imagined pain because most of the things that I feared during that time of my life never came to pass. I would sit there and imagine a lot of negative things. I think I could have stopped all this a lot sooner, but I didn't realize how important it is that our attitude (our change of attitude) can really change our life. I was convinced that if I could just change one person's view-point and have her come back and be with me that everything in my life would again be well. It was very controlling and manipulative, but it was where I was at the time. I wanted the love through one particular face and in the way that I was used to getting the love. Because I wasn't getting it the way I wanted, I felt that I wasn't getting it at all.

> I realize now that we don't ever fall out of love; the love just gets blocked, and blocked love creates pain, and pain renders us dysfunctional.

Love is eternal and it is always present, even if we can't feel it. We are all children of God. We might not know this consciously; we might forget it, but it can never not be a Divine creation.

Never did I dream, at the time when I was depressed, that there was a family (so vibrant, so powerful, so large) waiting to embrace me and my children. There was no way I could have imagined it. Even though I had friends in the fashion industry, I had never been received by a community like the Cell Tech community. Now, most of the time when I travel on weekends, I tend to bring my kids with me, or at least one of them, because I'm away a lot of weekends. And this is my way of giving them a good time. We have fun; we travel by airplane; they meet other kids, and we get to spend special time together. We've been going to really great places. Everywhere they go they're embraced into these large families where they feel well received.

So as I was lying in bed (those evenings I probably never slept more than two hours in a stretch), I was in a very bad state. I would go into my office during the day and start looking through papers of who I was going to call for jobs. I had no motivation to go out and take photographs, because I had really been doing it the last few years just to support my family. My passion was gone. *In fact I didn't know how to turn my pain into a passion.* There was nothing that I was passionate about except my children. And I used to sit there and think to myself–how am I going to get out of this hole?

Then something amazing happened. I have a cart with wheels in my office that has three baskets. We get them at a home office depot. You can keep papers and things in an in-basket and out-basket. If I was sitting I could touch it with my arm. I had papers in one of the baskets and I had books in another. You'll never guess what was in the top basket. Has anybody got an idea what was in the top basket? Tapes! I probably had a dozen opportunity tapes that people had sent to me in the mail. When I first moved back to America I had gotten involved in network marketing. I had seen an ad in the paper saying something about residual income. I knew something about residual income because I had friends who were artists, rock and roll stars, or movie people.

My sister is a very well known photographer and author, and is married to Kurt Vonnegut who is a wonderful, successful writer. Her name is **Jill Krementz** and she has created a number of wonderful books on her own. You might know them. She has books called *A Very Young Gymnast* and *A Very Young Rider* from her *Very Young Series*. And also **How It Feels To Fight For Your life** and **How it Feels When A Parent Dies** from her *How it Feels Series*. These books contain beautiful photographs of young kids with sensitively written testimonials and first person narratives. I knew she was doing very well selling these books over the years. The same was true of my friends that were artists. They would create works of art that would then build them residual income.

So I knew about this concept and appreciated it. I had never heard of network marketing in all my years in Europe, so when I read this ad there was something about it that really attracted me. I went to a meeting. I was living in California at the time, and this guy drew circles over everything. He talked about *five* people– get five people and you have 125 people, and then you have 500 people. Then you're sipping pina colada on the beach somewhere in Tahiti and you're making money while everybody's making phone calls.

I wasn't too impressed by the idea of selling phone sub-scriptions, but when I went home I couldn't sleep that night because the idea that I could have a thousand people in my life actually working while I was doing something else, really intrigued me.

As I came here today I spent time in the plane and had a really good trip. I read and wrote using my computer. I know that I've got literally thousands of people making phone calls. There might have been two to five to ten thousand hours of phone calls made in my organization today. I don't even know how many new people were added. I don't even need to worry about it anymore. So the visualization of a reality that I dreamed about those ten years ago actually came to pass. It took a long time, but I love this idea. I spent years looking at different companies. I tried selling discount telephone rates; I tried diet cookies; I tried gold and silver jewelry, and until I actually discovered Cell Tech I had had some moderate success, but I'd never had any of the kind of success that I have had in Cell Tech.

> **I think it's really important that the actions we take are in harmony with who we are and who we want to be.**

When I take certain actions, if those actions aren't in alignment with my higher self, I can beat my head against a wall, but those actions aren't going to be fruitful for me.

I did many things in trying to share networking opportunities and people always said, "Wow! You're really exciting and we love the idea of networking, but selling jewelry or selling telephone or diet cookies just doesn't do it for us." But I was saying, "Just do like I do. Sell lifestyle until something better comes along." I never really created a lot of momentum. I don't know if any of you have ever felt what

I felt when I joined Cell Tech. When you joined Cell Tech did you feel there was a big vacuum that just drew you into it? You could almost hear the sucking noise? Well, I felt that when I joined Cell Tech I plugged into a consciousness that was more than just my own.

Let me go back a little bit. I'm sitting there at my desk, depressed and wondering how I am going to get out of this hole, and I remember a story. There's a lady who lives in a little rural town and a flood starts to come. The rivers start to rise in this town. The water comes up to just about the level of her doorstep, and a man comes by in a rowboat and he says, "Mildred! Mildred! Get in! Get in! I'll take you to safety." And she says, "No! I think the water's going down. I'm fine; I'm fine." A couple of hours later, the water is up above her first story. She's on the second story and another boat comes by, and says, "Mildred! Come on and get in the boat." She says, "No, I've got too much stuff here. I think the water's going to go down in a minute. I'll be fine." Then she's up on the roof when the third boat comes by and she doesn't get in the boat–she dies and she goes to heaven. When she gets to heaven she looks and she says, "God, I don't understand. I went to church every single Sunday. I taught Sunday school. I was a good mother. I was a good grandmother. I did everything by the book. And when I had my first big challenge you didn't save me! What happened?" He says, "Mildred, I sent you four boats!"

What happened to me is the same. I kept saying to myself, "God, why am I in such pain? I've been a good father. I'm a good husband. Why do difficult, challenging, bad things happen to good people!" Little did I know that each day all I had to do was to reach into my basket. I had the tapes for months (I think I had 10 to 15 tapes; I'd never really counted them). In other words, the solution to all my challenges was right there but I didn't recognize it. It was only a few feet away, right within arms reach.

> **We all have windows of opportunities surrounding us at all moments, that we actually don't recognize.**

It's like the person who loses a piece of gold and walks right by ten piles of silver because he's just looking for the gold. I thought about this for months afterwards. What made me pick up the tape the day that I picked it up? If I could figure out what made me pick up the tape, maybe I can get some other people to pick it up too! I've mailed out tapes that haven't been picked up–not yet anyway. And so I did pick up the tape and like I told you at the time it didn't seem like a very important gesture.

> **A small gesture can make such a big effect as it leverages out.**

That's the whole concept of our business–when you leverage something out. If I was to stay where I'm pointed now and start walking I would be going in one direction and I would end up in the middle of the wall, but if I make a slight alteration now, just turn a few degrees, then I will walk directly to the door. If I don't make a small adjustment when I get to the middle of the wall, it takes a lot more energy to change direction, walk along the wall, and then out the door. So a small adjustment now saves me a lot of effort down the road.

The reason that I picked up the tape was because it had a name on it that I recognized. The name was Kare & Charles Possick. I had never met the Possicks, but the Possicks had written me letters for over eight years. They had written me letters about–*come on a cruise and learn about networking*; they had written me a letter about–*buy our mailing lists*; they had written me letters about tools to improve my networking business. I was just on a mailing list and the Possicks just never let up. I think every two or three months I got a letter. It got to a point where I didn't even open it when I saw the name, because I knew I would throw it out. I don't think that Charles knew what would happen when he sent me the first letter. I don't think he had the intent: "Oh boy, Tony Kent, Santa Fe, NM. I'm going to get this guy for Cell Tech." He didn't even know Cell Tech existed! Yet I turned out to be probably 25-30% of Charles' business. It was one of the best things, probably, in terms of recruiting he ever did, and he did it unconsciously. But he did have an awareness of what he was doing, and his intent was to be persevering and to be consistent. In order words, just because I didn't answer didn't matter. I don't know what he does to keep qualifying people, but he sent me letters for eight years, and it's probably going to make him a lot of money in his life; *just because he was persistent and consistent.* And he didn't know what he was doing when he started directly in relation to Cell Tech any more than I knew what I was doing when I picked up the tape. I'd love to stand up here in front of you and say, "Oh, I made this incredible decision. I was so smart to find Cell Tech." It was really in spite of myself.

So... I took that tape, put it in my car, and listened to it. It was the original Ray Cassano tape, and I thought, "This is great! I'm going to eat a *BG bite*; I'm going to go to heaven! My life is all going to be fixed!" I was really excited. I was a 30 year vegetarian and it made a lot of sense to me when I heard them talk about minerals, quality, and everything else. In fact, I was eating minerals, trace minerals, amino acids, ginseng, and spirulina. My medicine cabinet looked like a shelf in the local health food store. My icebox was full of bottles, and I had powders everywhere. I also had massive heartburn, indigestion, and gas from eating all these things. But I didn't know. They said it made you feel better. But it never addressed the cause of why I wasn't feeling good in the first place. And that's what really attracted me to the algae. They talked about addressing the cause of why I was tired. They talked about making connections; they talked about eating a wild-crafted food deep from the womb of nature. They talked about eating something from an ecosystem that was the richest biomass on the earth. They talked about something that was holistic and pure and clean: that it was made by God and not put together by some scientists in a lab who thought that a combination of this and a combination of that would be good for my system. It felt to me like there was a lot of truth in what I was listening to.

I came home and called up Kare Possick and introduced myself and said, "Please don't talk to me about the business opportunity. Don't talk to me about network marketing because I've already done that part, but I just want to eat this stuff and that's all I want to do." She said, "No problem." She was really warm, loving and accommodating. A few days later my package came. It wasn't quite as pretty as our new *EAT kits*, but it was a good package. It was the original *Sure Start* package that consisted of acidophilus, enzymes, Alpha and Omega. Does everybody in the room understand what those four products are? Anybody that doesn't? Don't be bashful. Good. I started the program like I was told to do. I started taking some enzymes and some acidophilus. A couple of weeks went by and I was up to four Alpha and four Omega, and had accelerated the program as I tend to do. If somebody had asked me if I was feeling any different I would have had to say, "I can't notice anything." I was probably so depressed at that time you might have hit me in the back of the head with a sledge hammer and I might not have noticed that either. I wasn't really into subtle differences in my body. I was just trying to exist from moment to moment and hour to hour.

Health is a lot more subtle than sickness.

One morning I was changing a pair of trousers, and I reached in, and was taking things from my pockets and transferring them to the new trousers, and I found an unopened tube of antacid tablets. I thought: wow that is interesting, because I realized when I took it out of my pocket that it had been in my pocket all week and I hadn't even opened it. It was a very strong revelation, because what I noticed was that health is a lot more subtle than sickness. In other words, I had had heartburn for four or five years in a row. I was taking five to ten antacids a day. The heartburn would go away, but was not stopped from coming back. So it was fixing the problem but it wasn't curing the cause of the problem. Because I wasn't having any heartburn I had totally spaced it. It wasn't like: Oh the algae's gotten rid of my heartburn, or the enzymes, or the acidophilus. I wasn't even aware that I wasn't having heartburn because I wasn't thinking about it. This was a big lesson to me because as I introduced the algae to hundreds of other people, there were many people who told me they didn't notice anything different, and I remembered to say–I didn't notice anything different, yet there were a lot of differences.

I was impressed with that, and started thinking about it all day, and it was a Friday. That Friday night my kids wanted to go see a movie. Now, going to a movie with dad at that time, meant that we would get into the movie, they'd get loaded up with popcorn and soft drinks, and we'd sit down. I'd have one kid on either side, and they would kind of keep tabs on me because when my head got down too far and my snoring got too loud–whap! I'd get the elbows so they wouldn't be embarrassed. I think when you're in a depression the first thing you tend to do when you relax is to fall asleep. I decided that night that I was going to try a new experience. I was going to try to actually watch the movie. So I took four more Alpha and four more Omega at about 6:00 o'clock and off we went to the movie. We get to the movie and all of a sudden we're through the trailers, and the commercials; and we're actually into the movie, and I notice my kids heads keep turning to look at me, and I wonder, "What are they looking at? Have I spilled popcorn?" I didn't even have popcorn. I hadn't even bought any. I wasn't hungry. I couldn't believe this! So, then I realized: Oh my gosh, I'm awake! I'm conscious! I watched the whole movie without falling asleep. This was a new experience after a number of years of having not done that. We used to get movies on video and I'd drive my kids nuts because every fifteen minutes they'd have to rewind it because I'd missed a part.

I went home that night and got the kids to bed, and then I was remembering some of the things said in the tape. I found myself walking around my office, and I wouldn't say, like the people on the tape, that I was vacuuming my house, but I was arranging my office. I would take papers from one pile and walk over and put them on another pile. I was walking around not knowing what I was doing but I was alert, and it was getting to be 11:00 o'clock and 12:00 o'clock at night. While I was moving all the papers I started to think about the algae, and I said, "I'm going to check out this stuff." I went to get my box that everything had come in. When I did that I discovered the book, *August Celebration*. Has anybody here not read this book yet? I started to read this book, at about 12:00 midnight, and what was amazing (and this is really the truth from my heart) when I read this book was that I finished it that night, and I knew in every cell of my body that my life was going to be changed forever. I didn't need anything more than the experience I'd had that day and what I experienced in this book. As I got involved in Cell Tech and built my business, this was the book that I used like a thermometer. Originally when I joined this was not part of every EAT kit, so people didn't get it. But the moment I thought somebody had a potential to be interested in the business, I almost always made them order the EAT kit plus this book. I'd jam it down their throat like a thermometer and if they came up hot I knew I had a business builder. If they came up cold, I knew that it wasn't the time yet. I didn't discard them or anything. I knew if they weren't jazzed by reading this book, that was not a problem, but I didn't find a single person that built a business under me that wasn't absolutely in love with this book. I've read it many, many times since then. I really, truly do love this book and as I read it the second, third, fourth, and fifth time it became a lot more fun because I started to know a lot of the people. I had met Showshawne, I had met Kim Bright, I'd met Katherine Clark.

Talking about little gestures that can sometimes change futures, think about Showshawne sticking his foot in Kim Bright's door so she can't close it on Thanksgiving Day. If she had closed the door she would have closed the door on an amazing future for herself. It was a small opening that Showshawne had, and he went through that opening. I think the last I heard was that Kim had 275,000 people in her downline. And Showshawne probably had even more because he got his foot in the door, because he made a little gesture. That's not a big gesture. I mean I can do it. You can all do it. If you're eating algae you can put your foot in people's doors. You just have to have the power of belief and conviction that Showshawne had.

Now remember, when he started he didn't have the belief system of 300,000 people with him. It makes a big difference to be part of a collective group where when you put your foot out you've got 300,000 people putting their energy with you. Showshawne was all by himself. Not that many people even knew about algae yet. So the gesture he made—it just shows how one person, one individual can change mass consciousness. Look at what Gandhi did with India. He brought the biggest empire of its time basically to its knees—a small, frail guy who, I think, weighed 95 pounds. And he did it by spending most of his time on his knees.

It's not that he had to take big, violent action. He just had to take action that was in harmony with who he was and what his purpose in life was. And that is really a lot about what I've come to share with you this weekend.

How many people here (raise your hand) have a written, memorized purpose statement. Not goals. Three people, four people out of a hundred. This is a normal percentage and wouldn't you say that that's the most powerful tool you have in your life? I mean, if people were to ask me, "Tony, what did you do to build such a big business?" I would say, "I knew what I wanted to accomplish, and I knew why I wanted to accomplish it." That is the single most important gesture that I think you can do, not only for your business but for your life.

I think a lot of people don't know how to listen to their heart, that's why so few people actually even do it.

They don't hear that voice because they don't know how. If somebody shows you the way, it makes a lot of sense to do it.

> **I don't believe that you can have a big business, unless you're a big person yourself. You can't have a business larger than you are because you won't know how to contain it.**

If you don't know how to relate to people in your personal life, you're not going to know how to relate to people in the business. You need to work on yourself if you want to have a big business.

> **Global transformation starts with personal transformation. You can't change the world if you don't know the mechanism to change yourself.**

You can't inspire people if you can't inspire yourself. So basically what I share with most of you tomorrow, (and what I will share in this book) is much more inner work.

Tonight I'm going to tell you what happened to me emotionally when I was exposed to the algae. Tomorrow is what happened in the business aspect. It's what happened the next morning after I read that book and I called up and I got Charles Possick on the phone. I'm going to tell you how I built my business step by step. The second hour we will write a purpose statement. I've devised a system with the help of many people, where everybody that comes tomorrow will walk out with a written purpose statement. It is the single most important thing you can offer yourself. Even if you don't intend to do the Cell Tech business, you should intend to come just to learn this. I think it's worth untold riches for your inner life. In the afternoon, we will spend time deciding actions and goals that are in alignment with this purpose, that you can use to build your Cell Tech business. We don't talk a lot about what do you say to so-and-so, or how do you do this, or how do you write a letter; this is bigger stuff. Once you know how to do the bigger stuff, once you know the why, the how becomes really easy. And I could tell you all an action that works for me, and every one of you could walk out of this room and have a different experience with that action. Just the same way I could tell you what amount of algae I personally eat, and every single one of you could have a different reaction or a different feeling from eating a different amount. We are all of us unique individuals. And what I come to share with you is to get you in touch with what you probably already know. There is nothing that I say that is particularly original or creative. I've read the same books you've read. I've been to the schools. I've been to the school of hard knocks in life; it's just that it's synthesized into a way that I think works especially for people that are interested in and drawn to the algae experience. I think it's true that the algae is the magnet that draws caring people. As I've gone to hundreds of people across America and Canada, I've realized that we all have one thing very archetypal in us, that is: that we all want to be of service. Everybody that's drawn to the Cell Tech experience seems to want to serve some kind of a higher cause.

> **I think one of our biggest fears is to lead a life that doesn't have meaning. To lead a meaningless life or to not lead the life that we think we're destined to lead is a very, very painful thing for almost everybody.**

I know, because of all those nights that I lay there awake in bed, worrying in fear, and just down on myself, and saying, "How could I be in my 50's and have accomplished so little?"

In fact I'm going to tell you a story. I usually tell this on Saturdays, but I feel to tell it now. I have had another big loss in my life. This was when my younger brother died in an accident. When I went to meet my parents to try to deal with this challenge, I realized that there was no material thing that I had, that could help to ease their pain and their suffering. I felt so spiritually inadequate that I couldn't comfort them and that I couldn't help them with their pain, that I went back to Europe. I completely left the photography business, and I went to India to look for different teachings and difference masters. On one of these quests I was in a little village, in the foothills of the Himalayas, and I was on my way to have a meeting with a teacher that I revered. We stopped in town and it was pretty sophisticated because it had a restaurant, and the restaurant actually had a covered outhouse, so that was really, really sophisticated. I went out to the outhouse and I was happy because I was in the woods but there was actually a cover. When I went inside it was almost blissful because in the hole in the ground right next to it there were all these magazines and newspapers, so I didn't have to use leaves. So I'm sitting there and I'm contemplating the universe as we all do, and I take some of these papers and I crumple them up to make them soft. Something (I don't know what it was), but something in my consciousness made me want to open the pages. I opened them and what did I find myself gazing at? A double page photograph that I personally had taken in El Magazine, now a piece of toilet paper in India. Do you know how that made me feel about right livelihood?

The Cell Tech experience has a deep, deep value to my life because I know I'm changing peoples lives. Not that that doesn't make a contribution, but it wasn't the contribution that I intended making. I feel much more empowered to come out and teach people how to get in alignment with their purpose.

Chapter Two
=====

The Heart of Network Marketing

M y passion for network marketing is because I feel
I completely understand its heart. The following
article is a rewrite of an article that was written for Diamond
Net, a newsletter published by the Possicks.

I Am Proud To Be A Networker

I remember when I first started out in network marketing
that I felt tongue-tied when people would ask me what I did
for a living. I was always struggling to come up with some
impressive and clever statement that would create enough
interest that I would be able to start to share my opportunity
with the person asking. I would say things like, "I'm in the
health and wealth business," or "I teach people how to create
residual income," or "I help guide people to financial freedom," etc. Now, I just say, "I'm a networker." And I want to
share with you what that means to me.

I believe that one of the key ingredients to building my
organization to 16,000 people in 16 months is that I really
love networking. And I love it with a passion. A lot of us
have an opportunity and don't really capitalize on it. Why is

that? Every one of us that works with the company has the same tools available to us, so what makes one person more successful than another? I believe it is passion, and I have a passion for my company, their vision, their products and network marketing. I have finally found a company whose vision harmonizes with my own, and I can express the totality of who I am. I have worked in other networking companies, but I never had as much success as I'm having now because my passion was never as complete, and there were always some areas I held back. I believe you have to be as proud of being a networker as you are of representing your company and sharing their products. It seems that in the other companies I either wasn't really passionate about the product, or maybe I never felt in alignment with the company vision. The result was that I never felt like taking big action steps and I didn't have the same level of faith that I have now. When I encountered challenges I couldn't manifest the energy I needed to create enough momentum to go through the blocks. If you look at your business and feel that in some areas you're stuck, my guess is that you'll see that your love is blocked in this area. If you hate follow-up, chances are you will be weak in this area. And if you don't love networking, you will be weak in sharing the opportunity with others. If you don't feel passion, how can you awaken others to be passionate? If you are having trouble finding builders, look at your own passion for building. Is it contagious? I believe mine is.

> **The company co-founders say that the greatest human need is the need to feel connected, and networking is about connecting.**

They also said that not only is networking safe as a form of business, it is essential, because it will redistribute the wealth into the hands of caring people. To be successful you must first help others, for without others being successful, you can not succeed. Networking is about collaboration, not competition. There is no discrimination, for you can be of any color or creed, any height or weight, from any background, and with various degrees of education. And it is a powerful path for personal growth.

You owe it to yourself to become as knowledgeable about networking as you are about the company's products and the company vision, because they are all linked together. I think that almost everyone involved in network marketing has had a certain percentage of people react with some kind of negative attitude when the idea of network marketing or MLM comes up. One common thought is: "Is this one of those pyramid schemes?" What I have found is that as my passion and success grows, I get very few negative responses, but people generally seem to fear that which they don't know, so I believe that the reason people might not be attracted to our business is simply that they don't know anything about it. The next time someone asks you, "Is this one of those pyramid things?" you can say something like, "I don't know; is this Egypt?" or you can simply ask, "What do you mean?" When asked what they mean, I find people express a really unclear idea, and this gives me a chance to explain a bit about how I see our industry. When I share with people that, "I'm a networker," I then usually ask if they know what that means, because more often than not they think it has to do with computers. I prefer asking a question back of someone rather than answering in a defensive manner, because there is a more harmonious pathway of communication that opens up. So here are a few relevant facts and ideas about our industry that will hopefully help you understand about our business, and in turn be able to educate others.

> **To me networking is what we do naturally when we want to share something we love with someone we love.**

It is the purest form I know of free enterprise and a way of doing business that honors each individual, simply because it allows everyone the opportunity and freedom to be the best they can. Currently one of America's fastest growing industries, networking is the perfect place to live the purpose of helping others achieve success in their lives.

I ask people if when they see a good movie or read a great book, do they keep this to themselves or do they share it with their loved ones; and when they say they share, because they almost always say they do, I can say, "Well, you're what I would call a natural networker." Then I explain how they don't get paid for sharing this information, at least I don't. When I recommend a restaurant to friends, the restaurant doesn't give me a free meal, but that Cell Tech does pay me for sharing information about a product that I really love. Then I ask, "Do you like to sell?" and if they say yes, I say "Great, you'll love networking because it makes selling fun and easy, because it is more about sharing than selling, so it makes the hard sell softer," and if they say no, I say, "Great, because networking is about sharing and not selling."

Often I will ask people if they like alternative medicine, or alternative education, because if they do I often find they are the kind of people drawn to some level of the opportunity I share. If they say no, I ask them why; but when they say yes, I simply say that networking is an alternative way of distributing product to the consumer, thus it is an alternative way of doing business. I then outline how Cell Tech has no middle men to pay because the product is only distributed by the distributors themselves, thus we also get to share in most of the profits. Network marketing companies pay a commission when people introduce their products to new people, and they continue to pay commissions as people continue with their use of the products.

I read that Mark Yarnell likes to ask people if they can retire before they die, and then shows them his opportunity to do this very thing.

There is a story that illustrates the concept of duplication in our business that I love. It goes something like this: One day a man was standing by a lake in India. It was the first day of the month and there was a water lily floating on the water. His guide explained that every day the water lilies would double, until at the end of the month, the lake would be completely covered with water lilies. The most amazing thing for him was that the day before the end of the month the lake was only half covered.

This is similar to the idea of a penny doubled every day for 30 days. At the end of the first week, you have $1.28. At the end of week two, you have $163.84. And now the fun starts. The small, almost insignificant penny at the end of week three, doubled every day, grows to $20,971.52. After week four, or 28 days, an unbelievable $2,684,354.56. And the last two days 5 and then 10 million dollars. The first time I grasped this principle I couldn't sleep for days.

I was introduced to network marketing principles through an opportunity in telecommunication sales, and the idea of making a few pennies on thousands upon thousands of calls took my breath away. The idea of compounded interest created through duplicating myself in network marketing, and thus creating residual income exploded every idea I had ever held about financial freedom and security. Not only did you create incredible income, as your income accelerated and grew so would your free time. I had always seen that people who created large businesses usually became slaves to their own growth. But in networking, the more people you help to grow successful businesses, the more free you actually become, because you have taught them how to do the business. And you can't become successful in network marketing unless the people under you have some measure of success. Isn't this the way it should be?

> **Your success is directly proportionate to how much you help others.**

I would like to quote a paragraph from one of my favorite books, *Being the best you can be in MLM*, by **John Kalench.** "Network marketing drives people towards their destinies. It naturally accelerates your learning curve. It enables you to grow as a person faster and farther. It enables you to accomplish more and to contribute more to yourself and to your world. Network marketing is a system that provides you the opportunity to leverage your unique God-given creative abilities to have a dramatic, beneficial impact on the lives of hundreds, thousands, or even millions of other people! And it does this by virtue of its own inherent, powerful and inspired natural design."

Most people stay in corporate America for job security, yet last year over one million white collar workers were laid off....that's 2,777 per day. Corporations are too busy trying to survive themselves and there are more than 9 million jobless Americans; victims of change they can't control. Through our own home based business we can regain control of our lives by taking responsibility for ourselves.

Another thing that I love about our business is time leveraging. In other words, before I traded time for dollars. I worked as a fashion photographer, and when my day was booked for one client that was it. I couldn't sell the day twice. So if I wanted to make money, I had to trade my time, and there are just so many hours per day I can trade. If just a small percentage of my network just works one hour a day, say 1000 people, that's 1000 hours of work that get accomplished. If I was to work myself these thousand hours that's over three months of ten hour days, seven days a week.

Cell Tech's co-founders chose network marketing because like the product, it is clean and pure and offers hope to everyone. I believe that if you knew what I know about network marketing, you would have the same passion for it that I do, and this passion would help to open the hearts of countless others to the truth, integrity, and magic of our industry. So study everything you can, subscribe to Upline 800-800-6349 (my favorite monthly newsletter, full of wonderful resources), and the next time someone says what do you do, tell them with love and passion in your heart that, "I'm in network marketing."

Chapter Three

Self Empowerment

One of the reasons I have been so fortunate with building a large organization is because of the people that joined my team. The highest current status in Cell Tech's marketing plan is that of Double Diamond and that means that each Double Diamond has created at least 5 Executives (means minimum of 20 people) on their first level and a total of at least 20 Executives in their organizations. I have been blessed with 8 Double Diamonds on my first level.

I went to a seminar once in Los Angeles given by Gilles Arbour, a Canadian Double Diamond, and he mentioned that one friend of his, Harriett Fels, a Double Diamond on his first level, had earned him over a million dollars in commissions. He smiled and said, "Maybe I should send her one of those American post cards that says, "Thanks a Million."

I have also been helped by many other leaders in Cell Tech who so openly shared their wisdom, and this helped me to understand a lot of different systems other than the tape system. Elsewhere, especially in the transcripts, I tell the story of how a lot of these people built their downlines, so here I want to discuss much more the philosophy behind them. As I have said, *network marketing allows each individual to express their own unique gifts*, and every one of my lines has been built in a different way, with each person choosing to do what worked for them, rather than my imposing what I do or like to do. I always share what I like to do, but I was not responsible for creating their success. They were, and I am glad, because I like having people that accept personal responsibility.

> **It is said that a great leader is not the one with the most followers, but the one who creates the most leaders.**

I like to aspire to greatness within myself, and I like to accept responsibility for myself, for my successes and for my setbacks. It had never been my dream to create a network that I had to baby-sit. This does not allow for *time freedom*, which is one of the rewards of this business that I most cherish. Fortunately for me the people that became part of my team felt like I did. I think it's true, that like attracts like.

My momentum really started when Ron and Linda Kalvin, and Beverly and Tom McPeek both started building quickly. Ron and Linda liked the cold market tapes that I was using, and Bev and Tom were really natural networkers, and felt more inclined to start to build by word of mouth. We were all using the tape created by Ray and Kim Cassano, and were enjoying wonderful results. Some people mailed it out to strangers, others just handed it out to immediate family, others did some of both. In other words, everyone was doing their thing. So the McPeeks were mixing cold and warm market while the Kalvins started concentrating like I had on more cold market. In my case I felt like it was too soon to go to my warm market, it had been just a few weeks since I had so passionately proposed a different networking company, so I wanted to show them some success before I talked to them again. I think the Kalvins preferred the cold market, perhaps for different reasons.

So as early as February I started to feel some momentum, which got me really excited. There were some other people, Renae Van Thiel from Oregon and Vallerie and John Doell from Canada who also started quickly. As far as I am concerned success in networking really relies on being able to duplicate; in other words, being able to get people to actually start sponsoring. I have seen so often people with over 100 people in their organizations that have no one else sponsoring, and they get tired and discouraged quite quickly. In my company, many people actually boast about having really committed algae eaters, which is wonderful, but without business builders they don't have real growth. I have come to realize that these kind of people are stuck because deep inside themselves they have some reservations about network marketing as a business. Usually these folks are very product orientated and quite passionate about the algae and its reported benefits, and very good at transmitting this passion to others, but when it comes to sharing the business opportunity they do not have the same passion and so there is no fire in their belly when they talk about it. Because the business is not exciting to them, they are unable to excite others. They are, in fact, being very true to a part of themselves. Most of the time, I sense a lot of conflict with them, for they would like to have a bigger business, but their internal dialogue sends out such a contradictory message that they get stuck. One part of them wants more, another part says that they don't like "selling."

Personally I don't feel like I'm selling anything. I simply share the algae, the opportunity, and the vision with everyone I can. I have made a conscious commitment for my own personal growth to experience love with everyone I meet, and I share Cell Tech in the sharing of this love. I like to leave a lot of space to allow the person to do what they wish with this gift, because if I drag them into Cell Tech I know that I'm going to drag them along most of the time. Just like Charles Possick who knows that there are plenty of people who will fall in love with this opportunity, I don't feel I need

everyone I meet to get involved. I like to co-create with people who are excited and passionate about life, and who are
willing to accept personal responsibility for getting what
they want. I know there are lots and lots of people who
would love to have me build the business for them, but I like
to work with people who really love what they do.
Networking is like life, and there are challenges along the
path that I see as wonderful opportunities to find out who we
really are by how we react to these challenges. In the end if
we do too much for other people, we disempower them. I did
this frequently with my children until I realized what I was
doing.

We celebrate a lot in Cell Tech, Daryl always calls us
"The Celebration Company," and last year a lot of the distributors took a cruise together. During my first year in Cell
Tech I had worked so hard and such long hours I hardly had
any private time with my kids, so I took all four of them for
a week long cruise with fellow distributors, and then a week
on the island of St. Lucia. During this time I got to meet personally with a lot of successful Cell Tech Double Diamonds,
and I learned so much about what was working for them. It
felt wonderful to be with so many like minded people, and I
felt my vision expand enormously as my thoughts congealed
with theirs. I also enjoyed knowing that while I was away
vacationing, my business was growing.

During this cruise, I gave a small talk about how I had
helped my two older children build their business. When
Charles had told me towards the end of January I should start
creating executives, I started to put all my new leads under
Jason and Jessica. I told them I was going to do this, and that
until they decided to actually do the business I would ask
them to put their checks back into the business; but when
they actually started to build, then the check would be theirs.
Jessica, the older of the two, was very passionate about riding and was working very long hours at a nearby stable.
Jason was working in restaurants to earn extra income. When
they both became executive at the end of February, Jason

immediately got involved in building his own line, but Jessica seemed to have almost no interest. What was interesting is that without really doing Cell Tech, Jessica's business seem to grow even faster than Jason's, who actually was very committed. Jessica, however, put forth tremendous passion and energy into her riding, waking at 5 am almost every morning, at least 6, and often 7 days a week. It taught me that God doesn't always send rewards necessarily where we might expect them. In other words, I think that when we give we always receive, but we might give to *A* and receive through *B*.

During the cruise, both Jason and Jessica came up on stage during one of the group presentations and were applauded for both being Diamonds (the level just before Double Diamond). Afterwards Jessica spoke to me and said she felt really awkward being up there because she felt she hadn't really done much, but she also had gotten really excited now about the opportunity because after hearing Daryl and Marta speak and meeting all the Cell Tech people, she felt that she really wanted now to get involved. I understood then how easily we can make people feel disempowered even when we have good intentions. Six months later Jessica made Double Diamond, as did Jason, and it was totally due to their own efforts. They are now the two youngest double Diamonds in the history of Cell Tech, and I am genuinely proud of them. Sara Finnerty was only 23 when she made Double Diamond, and this is inspiring more and more youth to explore the business opportunity.

We have a mentoring program in Cell Tech where Debut Double Diamonds draw a mentor by lottery during our historic August Celebration, and five months later at her first Celebration Jessica drew Showshawne, the first Cell Tech Double Diamond. When he met her, he asked her what she had done to become Double Diamond at such an early age, and she said, "I guess I just allowed it to happen." His reply was, "I don't think I need to teach you anything."

> **Often we don't allow ourselves abundance. Success is more about being than it is about doing, which is why we are called human beings rather than human doings.**

An added footnote of success for Jessica.

Just last week (1/8/97) Jessica married Darren, who is a musician she met on the cruise. Darren became the 20th executive in Jessica's downline that qualified her for Double Diamond, and they are building their business together now. They just moved to San Francisco, where Jessica will work with a stable part time and Darren will continue with his music. They are both excited about the freedom that Cell Tech has allowed them to experience in their lives. Just yesterday we started working together on an audio prospecting tape for the youth market, and we had a wonderful discussion about the choices we make in our lives and how the quality of choices we make is reflected in the quality of our lives, which leads right into my next subject, which concerns choices.

Chapter Four

Choices

Right from the beginning in network marketing, the quality of our choices are going to deeply affect the quality of our experience.

Starting with the choice of company, the outcome of many events will be decided long before we experience any particular outcome. And more often then we think, some of our best results are obtained as a result of an action we took that was initiated with another result in mind.

Take the case of the Possicks and myself. I had spent the most part of my life living and working in France. When I returned to live in the United States in the mid-eighties, I went to an opportunity meeting in Los Angeles which introduced me to network marketing. When I came home that night, I had trouble sleeping. I had been introduced to the concept of leverage (more about that later), and I was deeply attracted to the idea that while I was sleeping or vacationing there could be over 1000 people working at some task for which I could earn residual income. How do you determine if you have residual income? It's quite simple. Stop working for three months, and if you continue to receive a check, chances are this is residual income. After this meeting I got involved. For a number of months, I spent my spare time signing people up to a new long distance service. I created a bit of momentum, got some people to come to one of the opportunity meetings, and somewhere in this process ordered some books about network marketing. Charles Possick, I believe, bought a mailing list from one of the people that sold me one of these books, and started mailing me letters offering his mailing lists, or a cruise on which I could network with industry leaders. Now when I bought whatever book I bought, this was a choice I made that was only partially conscious. What I thought I wanted at the time, was this book. I believe now that what I wanted was contact with the Possicks so that one day they would introduce me to Cell Tech. What Charles, I guess, consciously wanted at the time was that I become a client because he had not yet even heard of Cell Tech. I don't imagine at the time he looked at my name on a label and was thinking that here was someone who would wind up bringing over 16,000 people into his downline in 16 months. He probably never even saw the label. My point is that sometimes a small, innocuous decision to do something leads to enormous, unanticipated results.

Almost ten years after the initial letter, I reached into a basket full of tapes I had received in the mail, and chose the tape the Possicks had sent me. I spent months trying to recall why I picked up the tape that day (it had been in the basket for months), and then it dawned upon me that it was because I had recognized their name on the tape and all the other names meant nothing to me. What does it take to be successful in network marketing? Persistence and consistence, they say. Eight years of mailing letters to someone who never once responded personifies these qualities. I thought if I could figure out why I chose the tape that day, I would know how to guide other people to take the same action. I had lain awake for hours every night wondering how I was going to salvage my life, and every day the answer was within arms reach. I would pray to God for some answer to my pain, not aware that He had sent it months before. I wonder how many opportunities lay within arms reach that we don't recognize until we are truly ready. Sometimes we are so busy looking for gold, we walk right by all the diamonds.

The choice I made that day has affected my life so deeply, and now the lives of many others. And yet when I made that choice, to pick up the tape that day, I had no conscious awareness that my life would be impacted to such an extent. Every single moment of our lives carries within it this potential. I like the beauty of not knowing what result will come from a choice we make.

I was seeing a lady, Kathleen Loeks, during the breakup of my marriage, as a spiritual counselor, and she explained to me that before the breakup had occurred I was looking at a tapestry of my life with a really clear image where I saw myself as a father, husband, successful photographer, etc. and that this picture was very comforting. Now the threads of my life had come unwoven and there was no longer this image to hold onto. All the yarn had become unraveled and was lying on the floor, and it was frightening.

> **One of the big challenges in life is to have the courage to move out of our comfort zones where we feel secure, and expand ourselves by taking risks.**

There is truth in the statement that if we keep on doing what we've been doing we will keep on getting what we've been getting. As I grasped the meaning of what Kathleen was sharing with me, I felt I was free falling and had nothing to hold onto. Later I read a **Deepak Chopra** book and he was talking about the beauty of existing in a place of unlimited possibilities. When we can just be and not try to manipulate the outcome of any action, *just let go and let God*, we are then in one of the most creative places to be. So as I looked at all the threads of yarn on the floor of my life, I realized that I had a choice. I could weave the threads back into a comfortable picture where I felt secure and thus overcome my fear, or I could just let go of my fear and trust that God would weave a better image and do a better job than I had done. Once again, as always, I had a choice between living with fear or love. Having done so many things in my life that were motivated by fear, and my life having apparently fallen apart, I elected to try something different. Kathleen's husband, Derk, said I could look at the dark night of the soul as a place that was totally frightening, or I could look at it as the place where all great mystics go on their way to reuniting with the Creator. As I could not seem to change the unfolding of certain events in my life that were more about what someone else was deciding, I (wisely, I think) decided to adjust my attitude.

> **By changing my choices I could change my life.**

Another therapist I was seeing, Ava, told me my wife must be thrilled with all the free therapy sessions I was giving her, because I would show up and spend the entire hour analyzing her. I just kept jumping from one therapist to another with the intention of finding someone who would say I was right, it was all her fault, and when it didn't happen I was left with the fact that I better look at myself. That is when it dawned upon me that I couldn't and shouldn't try to control her choices, and better start looking at what choices I had, and accept that it was my choices, and not hers, that I had some say with. *I read a statement somewhere that the most important discovery of the past hundred years was that we could alter our lives by altering our thoughts.* This is one of those pieces of information that we know deep within ourselves and that we sometimes take a long time to acknowledge.

As I gradually started to accept that it was myself I had to look at, I also realized that even though I could not change Nathalie or get her to do what I wanted, I could initiate some changes within myself that would have profound changes in my life.

There were many times during those years I felt that it was not just me against her, or my ideas against hers. Some days I would have this feeling that there was something bigger in all this that I just couldn't put words to. Later, I discovered what it was. The picture that I was holding on to so strongly was that of keeping the family together. This is one of those huge, archetypal feelings that plugged into a part of the mass consciousness. One of our most primal urges is to feel connected through a sense of family. **Caroline Myss**, in her wonderful book, *Anatomy of the Spirit*, refers to this connection as Tribal Power, which denotes group energy, group identity, group willpower, and group belief patterns. When we plug into this, our personal power gets expanded by those other like-minded people. What I felt happened was that Nathalie was plugged into a different group consciousness, that of the women who were leaving the family environment to claim their independence, and a lot of her friends at the time were going through a similar experience. She also followed their methodology, which was to hire a lawyer, and aggressively pursue divorce. The reason I bring all this up is to illustrate a point. Sometimes when we have choices to make, we find ourselves gravitating towards a decision without understanding or consciously knowing why, and I believe it is because we are plugged into a group consciousness that we don't even realize we are a part of. When some days we wake up feeling fear, or discomfort, it is sometimes just a ground swell of emotion of our host group. So I am starting to pay more attention to what groups I am connected to by looking really closely at the different individuals that come close to me in my life. If I am emotionally connected with an individual, I want to be sure that I am not allowing my choices to be influenced by them and whatever

group they might be connected to, unless I really feel attracted in a positive way to them.

When I joined Cell Tech, I felt an almost immediate
change in my life, and I know this is because I immediately
plugged into a huge group of like minded people all focused
in the same direction that my deep self felt connected to.
When I connected to this new family, my children connected
with them through me, and I feel that this gave them a sense
of security also. Now when I make choices, I know that as a
leader in this company, the choices I make will affect thousands of other people, because many people now look to me
as an example, the same way that I look to others in my life
that I respect.

I often wonder what my spiritual teacher would do in any
given situation, and I know that through him I connect to a
huge group of other seekers and to his teachers, and to the
deep connection he experiences with the God force. Free
choice is God's gift to us, and what we do with this gift is the
gift we give back to God.

I have seen, so many times, people struggle with choice,
not knowing which way to go, and what works for me is really quite simple. The reason most people struggle with choice
is that they are not clear what their purpose in life is.

> **Once you know clearly what your purpose
> is, you just need to ask yourself which
> choice would be most aligned with your
> purpose.**

In other words, which choice would serve your purpose
the most. If we consistently make choices that we know are
helping us accomplish what we want most with our life, we
are going to feel good about ourselves and our actions. If we
are unclear about our purpose, we will make decisions that
leave us feeling insecure and not even know what's wrong.
The same holds true of certain actions, or goals in our lives.

We can beat our heads against a wall trying to accomplish some action and not get the result we are looking for, ending up feeling frustrated and stressed, simply because we are choosing actions that are not in alignment with our higher purpose.

During my seminars I always ask how many people have a written, memorized, purpose statement and up to now I have never seen more than five or six hands go up. So most people can't make choices in alignment with their purpose because they haven't yet made the decision of why they are here in the first place.

Once you have made a conscious statement, it is obviously easier to make choices that will place you in harmony with who you want to be; but until you know consciously who you want to be, I think you will spend a lot of time doing things that other strong minded people have you doing that helps them to what they want.

Similarly, most people either work for themselves and their own financial security, or they work for someone else and help them reach their dreams, frequently at the expense of their own.

We have a choice with every moment of our life, and that is to live that moment in fear or to live it with love. When we choose fear, we cannot live our purpose. It is only through love that we can do this. How can we know our purpose. That is the subject of the next two chapters.

Chapter Five
_____

Finding Your Purpose

Before I actually go into finding your purpose I want to share an article I wrote for the "Algae for All" newsletter.

When I went to the first training seminar I ever attended for Cell Tech, I met Harriett Fels, a lady who has become a very close friend. I was deeply impressed with and inspired by Harriett, and loved the way she constantly came from a place inside herself. All her actions seemed motivated by a sense of values that were in alignment with a high purpose, and during her talk she stated again and again that when you know why you are doing something the how will take care of itself. She called this "The Compelling Why," and that is what inspired the title of this article.

The Compelling Why or Identifying Dreams

One of the most commonly heard challenges in network marketing today is when your first level people tell you that, "I have a hundred people in my downline, but there are no real builders." What I have found in these cases is that the people who say this are not really clear themselves about why they are doing the business, and so it is hard for them to identify why others might want to really go for it. One of the first things I do with people I bring into my network is to discover what their dreams are, and what they really want to do with their life. But before you can do this I would suggest you identify your own dreams by learning to define what your own purpose is. A purpose is quite different from a goal.

> **A goal is something finite and attainable, like a new house and usually has a deadline for its attainment. A purpose is something that is ongoing and involves a cause that is much bigger than ourselves.**

It is my belief that a lot of the pain, fear and confusion of our lives is because we have not identified our purpose. We know that we are alive but we are not sure why. Modern technology has helped to make life more comfortable, but the apparent security of this comfort has allowed us to stop questioning the mystery of our existence. We have lulled ourselves to sleep.

Everyone comes into this life with the intention of being good, but as we develop our egos, our love gets blocked and with the blocked love comes pain, and with the pain comes dysfunction.

> **Violence is a way of lashing out against the sense of fear and hopelessness that is created when our heart is blocked in the expression of love.**

One of the most powerful steps we can take as an individual is to create a purpose statement, and this will help expand our awareness of why we are here.

You can start by writing out on a single sheet of paper what you believe you are here on earth to accomplish. A good purpose statement might start out as a paragraph, but as you develop a clearer idea of your purpose I feel it helps to refine your statement and end up with one powerful sentence. "I want to serve humanity" is really too vague because the statement doesn't reflect how you plan to serve humanity. So what you want to accomplish with this statement is a clear expression of not only what you would like to do but how you plan to do it. Once you have done this, you will find that all kinds of decisions become simpler, because all you have to really decide is which path would help further your purpose. When you know inside yourself that you have made a decision to do something because it will help you towards fulfilling your purpose, you will not feel that you are maybe missing some opportunity by not doing the other choice. Sometimes choosing relaxing and going to a movie over staying home and working could actually do more towards helping you reach your purpose because you will be recharging your internal batteries rather than over-extending yourself.

I have found that when I meet people I am really drawn to it is because I recognize in them a sense of purpose. When the purpose is really strong I don't even need to ask them what it is, because I can tell from their actions what their passion is.

Feel free to update and revise your statement on a regular basis. As you grow personally your purpose statement will change and grow also. And if you want to write out your goals, every time you set a goal ask yourself if attaining this goal will advance you towards your purpose, and this will help you with prioritizing your goals. When a goal is in alignment with your purpose, it will have a lot more emotional charge. If one of your goals is to own a boat and this doesn't really connect you to your purpose, I doubt you

would go after the goal with the same passion as if the reason you wanted the boat was to take underprivileged children out to teach them how to fish, because your purpose
statement included helping underprivileged children to learn
a craft. Once you have written out your own purpose statement you will find it easier to identify or help others identify what their purpose is.

*I believe that when your downline senses that you have
a strong purpose in your life, that you are not just out to
make money for yourself, that this in turn motivates them
and they start to reflect on their own dreams and aspirations.*

I was at a seminar recently led by Gilles Arbour, and
Gilles spent a lot of time helping people connect their values
to their monetary goals. He taught that money of itself had
no value, that what was important was what people wanted
to do with their money. If someone tells you they want to
make 1000 dollars a month, you should find out what they
want to do with that 1000 dollars, because they might not
have a clear idea themselves. And if they do have an idea,
like start a college fund for their children, you can then show
them how your opportunity can make that vision a reality,
and they will feel a lot more connected and motivated to take
some action steps. I am constantly surprised by the vague-
ness of people's objectives. When people are not motivated
to take action steps I find that more often than not, they have
no really strong compelling why.

A friend of mine, Harriett Fels taught me a lot about the
compelling why. Hariett has always had big dreams and a
sense of purpose, but when she talks about what got her to
take action steps to build her business, what it came down to
was that she really loved to have the freedom to stay in her
pajamas all day if she felt like it. She truly hated having to
get up early, get dressed, go outside in the freezing winter
climate where she lived, wait for a bus and go to work all

day for someone else. I feel that one reason she hated this was because it did very little to further her purpose. In fact, it probably held her back. So when you have people in your downline that are not motivated to action, sometimes gently helping them face the reality of how little they really love what they're doing, if this is the case, will be a gift for them. If we continue doing the same things in our lives, chances are we are going to continue getting the same results. If you can help people recognize that they want change in their lives, and you can learn what they really dislike about their current situation, you can also discover ways that will help motivate them to action. Don't try to get them to be motivated by what motivates you, because maybe a simple thing like not wanting to get out of their pajamas will be the key that works for them.

Not long ago I was in Reno, Nevada for a week-end masters seminar, and Richard Brooke from Oxyfresh was talking about how people usually have an intention or goal that is quite a bit bigger than their internal expectation. What I mean here is that often people will express outwardly that they would like to make 5000 dollars a month but internally they really only truly believe they will make a thousand, and the way he shared this with me was so powerful I would like to share it with you also, because I realized that there was a lot of truth in what he said.

First he asked us to write down a figure of what we would like to be making per month a year from today with our current company, and for purpose of this article let's take the figure of 10,000 dollars. After we had written this down, he then asked that we choose a figure that we were absolutely sure we would make, so sure that we would bet our life and our house that we would attain this figure. Now please realize that this is just an exercise and that you are not being threatened with having to lose something precious, but please just play along because the power of this process can really help you. So let's say we originally put $10,000, but now because we really want to be absolutely sure that we don't lose our business we put $4,000. The point here is that the $6,000 difference has a lot of importance, because when I did this exercise I realized that when I looked at the difference in the two amounts, I had very clear and precise places where I was going to spend my first figure, (our $10,000), but I had no clear places where I was going to spend the rest of the income. What happens here is very interesting, because when you intend to make $10,000 but only really expect $4,000, because this amount is really what your internal voice is telling you that you are going to make, you can make say $5,000 and be unhappy because your expectation was for more. If you were aware that your internal dialogue was really for $4,000, you would be really happy to exceed that by $1,000. The point I'm trying to make is that we let a lot of dissatisfaction creep into our lives because we compare results with dreams rather than realities. After I did this exercise I realized that all my life I had always made good money but that I had also never made more than I thought I needed. So I was constantly caught in those endless struggles at the end of the month trying to make ends meet. Even when my income doubled, I still spent everything.

What I realized in this exercise, and in my conversation later with Richard, was that if I wanted to increase my income, I really need to make more real the use I would have for the intended income.

So following his advice I decided to write out a one to two page story of what my life would be like when I was earning the intended income. The story started in the morning when I woke up and was going out to the mail box to get my check. I described what I felt like, where I lived, and the feeling I had when I opened the check. I then described walking back into the house, going into my incredible work space, feeling great, sharing the check with the person working with me, and than letting them take over the responsibilities of paying off all the monthly expenditures. I paid myself first, putting away 10% to use for fun, then another 10% for tithing. By the time taxes were paid and bills were caught up I still had some left over so I carefully allocated this money for use towards things that had value for me. I loved having the freedom of no worrying financially and then spent the rest of the time just writing a detailed version of what my day felt like. It has not even been a month since I did this and already there have been things happening that have helped increase my income significantly. By simply making the income difference more realistic I expanded the possibility of acquiring it, and as it became real in my thoughts it manifested in my life. Just as every object was a thought in someone's mind before it became a reality, just as this text was a thought in my mind before I brought it to creation, the more tangible something is in the mind, the more tangible it will become in the real world. So by actually creating on paper a life for this extra income, I believe I drew it out of creation and into manifestation.

So I believe that when you connect with those in your network, and you discover what their dream is, you can help them create a reality of their *compelling why* by sharing with them some of these ideas.

> **When they attach a value to their income, when they actually commit to writing what it would feel like to make this sum, you will have a much more committed business builder and a real partner in your business.**

They will feel you care about them because you share their dream. Once you help them really understand and feel the *why*, the *how* will happen by itself, because once you have them acting in harmony with their highest aspirations, they will live each moment with fuller integrity. Each decision will be easy to make because they will choose the path that will help them to fulfill their purpose. And because they will be acting with purpose, they will be acting from their heart and thus with much more passion. The doing will feel so good they will detach from the result, and then the field of unlimited possibility will be before them.

So next time one of the people in your network mentions they have no builders in their organization, start first with their commitment, let them really start by exploring themselves with your help, and once they have discovered how all these tools work for themselves then they should be able to duplicate the same process with the people in their network.

Now let's explore some more about helping to build a purpose statement.

Chapter Six

Building A Purpose Statement

I am often asked by people what I think is the key to my success, and I always answer that everything in my life comes as a result of my faith in God.

In terms of what is the most important action step, I would have to say it is in defining my purpose in life and getting a written, memorized statement that a child could understand. I have been blessed in that I have had some wonderful teachers along the way, and the system that I am going to share with you now is a blending of all of the information I acquired along the way.

When I first started leading seminars, I always tried to communicate to people the importance of a purpose statement. I think that one of our biggest fears is to lead a life without meaning, a life where we don't feel that we have made a difference.

> Unless we know why we are here and what our unique gift is, it is difficult to find a path of action where we feel we make a significant contribution.

All to often we get caught up in "existence mode" and then this develops into a pattern. Years go by and we never want to face the fact that we are on a course that leads to nowhere. When we are confronted by someone or something that comes in the form of a wake up call, it is frequently depressing because we feel we have been wasting our lives. When I would bring up this subject in seminars, after a while I realized that when people were confronted with the question of what is the purpose of their life, they would get stuck in a place that didn't always feel good. The reason for this is that for many people, it is a seemingly overwhelming task to put their purpose in clear and concise words.

I worked for a long time on how I could help people overcome this challenge, and I feel I have made some progress. I started by going to the bookstore and was astonished to find so few books about defining a purpose statement.

I read once that Steven Covey, one of the foremost teachers and motivators in the country, took eight months to define a purpose statement for his family. The reason for this is because there is a process involved, and a purpose is such an ongoing thing, rather then something finite, like a goal or a mission.

A goal or a mission is a thing that can be accomplished within the framework of a time limit. An example would be the goal of buying a new home by the end of the year, or within two years. A mission is something that is greater than a goal, and usually involves a cause. Ghandi had a mission of home rule for India, Kennedy had a mission of having the U.S. put a man on the moon. In a sense, a mission is bigger and more important than a goal, and is usually in alignment with a person's purpose.

A purpose is something that is bigger than we are, something that no matter how much or how often we do, there is still room for more. There is no limit to how much we can love or be loved, there is no limit to how much faith we can have, there is no limit to how much we can serve.

> **Purpose is something that comes from the heart, is full of passion, and fuels you so powerfully that no challenge is insurmountable. When you know your purpose, every choice you have to make in your life is simplified, because all you have to ask yourself is which of the things you are choosing between will help to further your purpose the most.**

Living without knowing your purpose is like driving without knowing where you are going. I know many times just taking a walk without any apparent destination can be a wonderful experience, but if you have an appointment with someone and don't know how to get there, it can be frustrating. When you know your purpose, it is a tool that will help you meet your destiny, and this is one appointment we should all want to keep. We are, each one of us, a unique individual; each of us carries a special gift and our life's journey is a path which points the way and guides us to knowing why we are here. The more clear we become about our purpose, the more defined our path, and as our inner path gains clarity, the outside path becomes more focused. We see more clearly where we are going because we understand why we are going there. Each action we take resonates with our inner life, and we connect with other people who are clear about their life's purpose, and because focused energy is so powerful, a few people with a sense of purpose can break through the inertia of a large collective consciousness that is drifting with no particular direction, or just resisting an idea whose time has come. That is why we have so many visionaries who have, by themselves, changed the direction of a nation.

The co-founder of Cell Tech is just such a man. With the power of his vision he attracted the people into his life that were necessary to help him reach where he wants to go. Starting with his wife, the two of them have touched hundreds of thousands of lives. There now exists a core group of people each with similar visions who can attain more as a group than each can individually. These people are seekers with a vision of world peace, a group of passionate and energetic people mutually interested in creating a team of socially conscious, environmentally aware, spiritually and physically healthy souls united together with the intention to draw others to support this vision. All of this came about because one person started with a strong sense of purpose and was motivated day after day after day to find a way to accomplish this purpose. Daryl Kollman has always hungered for world peace and had an inside knowing that there could not be peace while millions of people were starving. His desire to feed the malnourished people of the world led him to the algae called alphanizomenon flos-aquae in the Klamath Basin because he knew that this superfood was a tool that would help him towards the realization of his purpose. With all the challenges he encountered, it was the fuel of this sense of purpose that drove him to not give up, and today the company stands poised at the threshold of its greatness. It took Daryl and Marta over a dozen years to get the first part of their team, and then just a few years to increase by almost ten times. Because each year there are more and more committed and connected people joining in this vision, there will soon be a force big enough that the word of its existence will be heard and felt over larger and larger areas.

> **There are many people like myself that lie awake at night and wonder what happened to their dreams. They yearn for a sense of feeling connected, they are thirsty for a life where they can be part of a team where they can make a difference.**

They know that deep in their heart they are here for a purpose and they are desperate to know what it is and how to express it. They are tired of the struggle of their daily life and are tired and lacking energy because they are eating food that doesn't nourish them because it comes from depleted soil. When they are exposed to a large group of people that are connected through a sense of purpose, they are drawn to this experience because these people are so charismatic. People with a clearly defined purpose are like magnets, because they mirror something of our own potential greatness back to us. In them we see a spark that is bright because it accentuates our own darkness, and this sense of contrast serves to awaken us. Their knowing awakens our own, their love and passion serves to remind us of how glorious it feels to be passionate and loving ourselves, and gradually it becomes impossible to return to the station of our previous existence because now we sense its emptiness.

> **We are not taught in our schools how to define our sense of purpose, we are not guided to express the beauty of our individuality, nor are we usually rewarded for being different.**

Fortunately there are more and more educators offering alternative education, and I see a day coming where more and more parents will not only trust the process of a more creative system of education, but will demand it, because more and more young people are graduating from these systems and being examples that are like shining beacons of light to their contemporaries. My son Jason recently told me that at his university he was told that the colleges are seeking people that have been to these schools, where personal responsibility is taught, and the kids are free to study only that to which they are drawn. These individuals revere values and a sense of purpose more than an A plus. Personally, if I was looking to hire someone to work with me, I would rather have one individual who knew their purpose than a bunch of college graduates who weren't sure of why they were here on earth.

As the company grew, and more and more people realized the value of this superfood, Marta became more and more passionate about finding a way to get this algae to the third world and to the starving people unnecessarily dying from malnutrition. She launched the now famous Cell Tech Solution, which has had a powerful effect on the future of Cell Tech, because hundreds of people have gotten involved. Originally, the Cell Tech Solution was created with the intent of sending up to 10% of the annual harvest of the algae to these malnourished people. There are now solution projects in Cambodia, Nicaragua, Brazil, Guatemala, India, The Dominican Republic, Ghana, and South Central Los Angeles, just to name a few. Distributors gather together and propose these projects, and once approved by Cell Tech, algae is shipped to these less fortunate people. This has added to the uniqueness of Cell Tech, and made it a home where people can have the opportunity to make a real difference in the lives of others. What I discovered when I toured the country as a Relay 2000 trainer was that the people of Cell Tech all seem to want to serve in some way and that the Cell Tech Solutions were in alignment with their purpose in life. Thus Cell Tech became more than just another opportunity to make money, but more important to most of the people involved, it became a place where the money was earned through helping others and thus felt like right livelihood.

How can we discover our purpose and put it in writing? This is surely one of the most challenging and thought provoking issues that we have to deal with. Often we find it frightening to confront such large issues without the benefit of guidance, and what I want to share with you now is a system devised through studying with many different teachers, and I am apologizing before starting for not remembering all my sources and all the names of the people who have contributed to this process. I kept many notes over the years, but sometimes it seems so obvious when I am taking notes that I will never forget the source, but later this is not always true.

What I hope is that in learning this system yourself you will be able to pass it on to others and help them get more consciously on a path with clear purpose. In order for this to happen I will explain along the way why I do things in the order I do, but feel free to change and adapt things to suit you. I know that the people who have contributed to this process did so because they wanted to serve, and I cannot imagine they would be upset if you use the information as you see fit. I will mention their books where appropriate, at least those that I remember. My consciousness was brought to these issues initially by a man named Jack Neima with Success Motivation Institute in Waco, Texas. I taught and sold goal setting programs for them at about the same time I discovered network marketing. The two most important books that I used were *The Path* by **Laurie Beth Jones** and *The On Purpose Person* by **Kevin McCarthy**. So let's get started.

Start by making a list of what you feel are your ten best qualities and your ten best talents. Talents are things that you do well, like cooking, driving, gardening, writing, speaking, etc. while qualities are more about being. Some examples of qualities might be kind, generous, compassionate, patient, loving, etc. During this entire process it is important to not mentally filter any information. Anything that comes to mind should be noted down, and can be eliminated or discarded later. For now, try to remember every flattering thing that your mom ever told you. Be kind and love yourself a lot, and don't judge yourself harshly. If you have a hard time finding good qualities think of what your friends get angry with you about, and then look at the other extreme. If they call you nosy, write down that you are curious; because *every good quality taken to extreme can lead to a dark side, and every dark quality has an opposite side of goodness.* When you pick up one end of the stick you also pick up the other end.

Our path is to integrate all of our nature, to embrace every part of our being just as we need to learn to embrace each other.

If we are to find peace in the world, we must learn to love as God loves, that is, unconditionally. Then we will be a true extension of our Creator and we will be living in and from the love that created us. Global change starts with personal transformation, and personal transformation starts with personal truth, and will culminate in global transformation.

Once you have listed all your qualities and talents, take a moment and circle the two or three of each that you feel you use the most. In all of these exercises here the numbers are just an indicator, and do not need to be exact. You can circle two, or four, or whatever number works for you. The purpose here is to start making conscious choices. The reason I start with this exercise is that I want everyone to have a feeling of self-worth about themselves, and when they actually write down a list of their qualities and talents they are committing not only to this process, but also they are able to see in a material form that there are good things about themselves that contribute to their uniqueness. I do not state this during the seminars, but I believe this helps people feel more positive about themselves and helps their self esteem. I want people to feel the courage to stretch themselves when they write their purpose, and I want them to sense that each of us is divine and thus potentially great.

So many people allow themselves to be diminished by an internal dialogue that destroys their self confidence.

I like to use this part of the process to reverse the direction of this thinking. Also, you will see later how referring back to this step we can construct an action plan that will be in alignment with each person's talents and passion.

Once everyone has circled the qualities and talents that they feel they use the most, I have them underline the three of each that they would like to use more often. Some of these might be the same. For instance, maybe you circled "good listener" as one of your talents, and you would still like to use this talent more often, so you might underline it as well. The reason for doing this is that later it will help to make choices about what actions the person should take by knowing what they would like to draw out of themselves. When people are writing down their purpose, one of the ways to know if they are on the right track is to see if the attainment of their purpose would necessitate the use of these talents and qualities. If this is true, you know that they are in alignment with who they would like to become.

Once this stage has been completed, I use a method taught to me by Laurie Beth Jones in her book *The Path*. I really give thanks to her for this, because it was really the missing piece of the puzzle for me in helping people get so much closer to actually being able to get a statement on paper that would work for them. She shared the idea of using a list of words from which people could actually choose words that they could then use to write down their purpose. What had happened in some of my earlier seminars was that many people could not find the words to express such a profound idea as *"what is my purpose in life"* and when they couldn't find the words it left them feeling in a negative frame of mind about themselves, the process, the seminar and me. When you share this process with friends or loved ones, or people in your downline that you want to help, please realize that for many people there is a lot of fear about looking so deeply at their lives. As I said before, not many people rejoice at the idea that they might not have been doing as much with their life as they would like. When people start to beat themselves up about having wasted so much time, tell them that instead of feeling bad about themselves, they could choose to feel good that their inner selves have brought them to this opportunity for change.

Besides, people that are willing to change and are looking for personal growth and transformation are people who might discover, as I did, that networking is a wonderful platform for just this kind of new expression.

Here's how I share this process in my seminars.

I have three different lists of words that I project onto a screen and I ask people to write down a few of the words that resonant with their heart. I ask them not to worry or think about how they will use the words, but just if they are attracted to them, to make note. I am not going to print the whole list here, but I will suggest that you go and buy the book called, *The Path* by **Laurie Beth Jones**, which is available in most bookstores.

Here are a few of the words, that I see people choosing a lot, so that you get an idea of how the process works.

affect, affirm, build, connect, create, delight, dream, educate, embrace, encourage, enhance, enliven, excite, facilitate, heal, help, inspire, light, love, manifest, motivate, nurture, open, promote, realize, serve, share, support, team, travel, work, worship...

What you would do is circle the two or three words that you feel the most connected with, and that touch your heart the most. Then you go through a list of groups, or causes, and pick the one that most attracts you. Here are a few examples.

environment, family, homeless, youth, spirituality, people, human development, children, animals, the poor, sports, community service, gardening, women's issues...

The last list Laurie calls *"key phrase"* or value, and includes words such as the following.

God, joy, service, justice, being present (from Brian Biro) creativity, integrity, excellence...

Please remember there are a lot more words in *The Path*, and if you want the whole list, you might like to get the book. I have also added a lot of words to the list over the months, as people during the seminar would offer suggestions.

So what you do now is to go and try to write a short purpose statement using the words you have chosen. A few examples of statements that people have come up with during the seminars make up the next list. Laurie Beth also suggests keeping the statement so simple that a ten year old can understand it.

My purpose is to: live each moment joyfully...be a light that inspires others...be present always...help people help themselves...serve God by loving others...help children heal...educate others about health...

Have fun with this. My experience has shown me that very often, the more the phrases are shortened, the more powerful they become. I think that this is because the more you focus energy, the more powerful it becomes.

A special word of thanks to Laurie Beth Jones for her book, and for her team who helped come up with all the words.

Chapter Seven

Taking Action

During those years of struggle with the darkness within me, I became an expert at feeling sorry for myself. In looking back I can see now how the attitudes I kept choosing created the atmosphere in which I lived. Change seemed impossible, and it was because I didn't know how to change my attitude.

I was working at the time with a shaman and healer by the name of Martine Practel. Nathalie had seen his wife in a natural market one day, and was drawn to her charismatic presence. She spoke to her and got her phone number. I don't remember exactly how it actually happened, but after Nathalie gave me the number I found myself sitting in Martine's home in Pecos, and because of a small, seemingly casual encounter in a market, my life was again going to change dramatically. Martine, besides becoming one of my closest friends, had a profound effect on my spiritual life, and thus the rest of my existence. One thing I learned is that it isn't only the encounter that matters, but whether or not some action is taken.

It is action in addition to thought that manifests something concrete.

> **If vision is to become reality, we need to take some kind of action.**

I was coming home last night from Los Angeles on a plane, and I sat next to a lady with whom I started to talk. I was coming home a day earlier than anticipated, she was traveling a day late. As I talked to her, she mentioned she was being relocated from Santa Clara to Albuquerque by her employer of 25 years, and if she wanted to keep her job she had no choice in the matter. I asked her if she liked what she did, and she said she was looking for change. I shared my opportunity with her and left her with a tape. I pointed out to her that our meeting felt more than accidental and she agreed. Now this meeting will most likely vanish from her consciousness pretty quickly if she doesn't listen to the tape, but the small action of taking that tape and actually doing something with it could result in the opening of dramatic possibilities for her. What will make the difference is the action she chooses or the lack of any specific action.

Wayne Gretsky, the hockey player, once said, *"I missed every shot I never took."* The idea I want to share here is the basic concept of leverage, a concept that is one of the foundations of our industry, the concept which, when I first experienced and truly understood it, made it difficult for me to sleep for a while because I was so excited. Leverage, the dictionary tells us, is *the increased means of accomplishing some purpose.* Usually when people in networking talk of leverage it is in relation to how many hours of your time you can leverage. In other words, when I start out working in network marketing I have no one in my downline, so most of the time working in my business is done 100% by me. I say almost, because your upline, or sponsor, might be helping you. Then when I find a friend who joins my business, if we both work four hours, I have leveraged my four hours into eight. As I now have thousands of people in my organization, while I am writing this chapter, there might be over a thousand hours of phone calls being made which will increase sales and commissions for me. I have thus leveraged my time substantially, and this for me is one of the concepts that attracted me so strongly in my love affair with network marketing. When I was taking photos, when my day was booked, those hours were not leveraged. Ten hours of work was ten hours, and I was not paid for any other hours. So from this idea was born a basis of success in networking which is, learn to leverage your time.

There is a gentleman called Robert Butwin, who is a master at this. All master networkers are good with this idea, and they all do it differently. My upline in Cell Tech is a good example of this diversity. Jeff Kalnitz, in over ten years, has only sponsored around a dozen people into Cell Tech, but the people he chose to sponsor have in turn built him a huge downline. One of these people is Byron Schlagenhauf. Byron also sponsored few people, but among those few was Kare and Charles Possick, who have brought in over 80,000 people. Charles sponsored two other people beside myself, Robert Butwin and Pete Buntman, two long-time friends. As I told you earlier, Charles placed me under these two friends of his with the idea of helping them build their businesses. I can remember back a few years when I was in sponsoring mode, and both Pete and I were putting in 16-20 hour days with the intention of creating a lot of momentum. We would often try to call Robert for three way strategy sessions, and Robert was just as often out with his kids or playing basketball. Pete and I would allow ourselves to get pretty frustrated, and then it dawned on us that Robert was actually smarter than we were. *He had effectively leveraged his time through us and was free to follow his passions.* So while Pete and I were glued to the phone all day and all night, Robert was leading a stress free, enjoyable day while his business grew 50-75% each month. Robert was obviously very knowledgeable about the concept of leverage and using it to maximum advantage. I had seen other network marketers burn themselves out by building a downline and doing too much for many of their people. If you do the work for others, you disempower them. And then when you stop from exhaustion they don't know how to do it themselves.

Before Cell Tech I worked a program that was a Binary Lateral compensation plan. This meant that I only had two legs, and that after I sponsored one person in each leg, I had to sponsor everyone else under these people. I was really drawn at first to this program. The plan called for weekly payouts, and within a month I was getting thousand dollar checks. But the way a binary works is that in order to qualify for a check, you have to fulfill a minimum requirement of growth in each leg, otherwise you have no paycheck. When you develop the "binary limp," which means one weak leg, you could have 10,000 new people come under you in one leg and never get a check. This happened in the company I was in. Someone had sponsored one of the superstars of the company who was making five figures a week, but because he had never developed another leg, he was not receiving checks. Thus he had not truly leveraged his time. As in everything this had its good points and bad. It does mean that no one gets a free ride by just sponsoring one person, but at the same time it's not really fair, in my thinking, that someone brings in a person who earns millions of dollars for a company, and gets nothing.

Another thing I dislike about this type of compensation plan is that it is not truly residual income. If you go away for awhile and one leg stops growing, you no longer earn a check. Thus your downline could grow from 5 to 50,000 people without you earning a check. I have seen a lot of leaders in these binary plans work themselves to exhaustion trying to keep both legs alive and well, so even though it appears easier and quicker in the beginning, sooner or later you pay your dues. I like the more traditional plans, where even though you are grossly underpaid in the earlier stages, whatever success you attain is more durable. That is why I chose a company with a consumable product. When someone joins a company with a one time *buy-in* you are obligated to keep after new people for growth, where as in Cell Tech if no new people join I still get a check from the steady users of the product. I now shy away from the quick, easy money and am happy to know that what I have chosen will serve me over a long period of time, rather than an instant fix. This is what feels to me like more permanent leverage. I know that there are no guarantees in life, and my downline could one day disappear also, but the whole system feels to have more integrity to me and I feel more peaceful.

I heard a story once that apparently inspired the concept of leverage in network marketing. A man was standing in front of a lake in India, that had a particular kind of lotus blossom on it. This lotus blossom would double every day, so on day one of the month there would be only one lotus on the lake, then on day two there would be two, then four, eight, etc. On the next to last day of the month the lake would be half covered and on the final day, the entire lake would be filled with the lotus blossoms.

A similar story is told about a penny that is doubled every day. Look at the following chart and see how the penny really flourishes in the last few days.

This chart really sums up for me what happens in building a network. In the beginning growth doesn't seem to be that exciting. In fact, most people usually quit networking within just a few weeks, or months of getting to a point where growth really starts.

Penny Doubled Every Day for 30 Days

Day 1	.02
Day 2	.04
Day 3	.08
Day 4	.16
Day 5	.32
Day 6	.64
Day 7	1.28
Day 8	2.56
Day 9	5.12
Day 10	10.24
Day 11	20.48
Day 12	40.96
Day 13	81.92
Day 14	163.84
Day 15	327.68
Day 16	655.36
Day 17	1,310.72
Day 18	2,621.44
Day 19	5,242.88
Day 20	10,485.76
Day 21	20,971.52
Day 22	41,943.04
Day 23	83,886.08
Day 24	167,772.16
Day 25	335,554.32
Day 26	671,088.64
Day 27	1,342,177.28
Day 28	2,684,354.56
Day 29	5,368,709.12
Day 30	10,737,418.24

Chapter Eight

The Importance of Relationship

As in our lives, networking is based on relationships. Without people we can't have a downline, and the quality of our downline is going to be determined by the quality of people we attract to it. In turn, the quality of people we attract into our life is a reflection of who we are and who we want to be. If we want to attract loving people into our life, we should start by being loving. D.H. Lawrence wrote a beautiful poem called *Search for Love*, that goes like this.

> *Those that go*
> *searching for love*
> *never find love.*
> *They only make manifest*
> *their own lovelessness.*
> *Only the loving find love,*
> *and they never have to seek for it.*

The best way I know of to find a good partner is to be a good partner. This is based on the principle that the love you give is the love you get. My teacher and guide, Sidi Shaykh Muhammad al-Jamal ar-Rifa`i has taught me so much in this domain. Actually, he has taught me so much about every-thing. When I am with him, he reflects back to me my own potential. I can actually taste the Divine through his heart, and he carries in the everyday existence of the material world the quality of unconditional love towards which I aspire to experience and express myself. His ability to embrace everyone and everything with no judgment and no separation shows me that it is possible for a person in the human form to be capable of living and walking in total awareness. To experience this in the reality is, for me, more powerful than reading about it. To be accepted in this loving way and to be able to experience this unconditional love opens the possibility within myself to know that I can express this from within myself to my children and loved ones.

My experience has taught me that people treat people in their downlines in the same manner they treat people in their life. Kind, loving people nurture the people that they work with in the same manner they nurture people that they live with.

In a wonderful book called **Conversations with God** by **Neale Walsch**, there is a lot of mention of how we must actu-ally act out an intent in order to experience directly a feeling. Once the thought or feeling of loving people gets acted out and manifested in loving acts, the reality is experienced first hand. Otherwise it is just a conception.

I often have the intent of doing something with my kids, and many times I get caught up in some other activity and because they seem to be around a lot, I procrastinate actual-ly doing something. I think all the time about my kids, and I am always full of very loving thoughts and great intentions, so in my mind, I am a good father, and take great care of them. The reality is that I could do a lot more with them, be a lot more present and do more things rather than just have good intentions.

This same tendency can be seen in my relationship with my downline. I think about them a lot, am very grateful to have them in my life, yet I don't actually spend time doing things with them that might help them build because I am always busy doing something else. I can rationalize this by saying that this helps create strong, individual leaders who do not get co-dependent, but that is not the point. *The point is that it takes more than good intentions to make vision become reality. There needs to be some action steps.*

So the same weaknesses that I exhibit in my personal life are reflected in my business, and vice versa. The strengths that I have in my personal life are also the strengths of my business. That is why I agree that you can not have a business bigger than you are. If we want to manage a large organization, we need to expand our possibilities so that we can contain the hearts of all those involved. Building a large network can stretch us in many ways, and the more we are able to handle, the more we will be given. There are so many stories of people who won a lottery, or received large amounts of money that they weren't adequately prepared to handle, and I have seen this seemingly destroy their lives. Look at the number of rock stars who died so young, because of their inability to deal with fame and fortune. The inner work we do is crucial to being able to assimilate all the benefits that networking can bring to us, and as we expand inwardly we can also expand outwardly.

> **Relationships are not about obligations, they are about opportunities.**

When we are with another person, we have an opportunity to experience ourselves in relation to someone else. Sidi shared a saying with me that goes like this. *"I was a hidden treasure that longed to be known so I drew all of the creation out of myself in order to know myself."* So even God uses relationship to know Himself. He created something out of Himself in order to be able to look at and experience Himself.

Our life is made up of relationships. The quality of our health is determined by how one part of our body relates to another. When one part becomes dysfunctional, other parts are severely affected. If we lose our sight, our hearing improves, if one muscle grows weak, we compensate by developing another muscle.

Our downlines work in the same way. In order to have a healthy downline it is worthwhile to have your leaders build using different strategies. This will create variety and if one system slows down another will fill the gap.

In Cell Tech there was a tremendous growth spurt when Charles Possick started sending the Ray Cassano tape to cold market names. There were many who built using this system exclusively, and when the current batch of lists was used up, there were many people who had not developed any other systems in their organizations and so they had no way to grow. In our personal relationships, unless we grow into multi-faceted individuals, our relationships will also stagnate. The more we grow personally and the more we learn to nourish ourselves, the more we can nourish others.

Early in my career as a photographer I had a lot of difficulty giving directions to models in a studio setting. One night, after a session, when the studio was empty, I went out on a set with just a white paper as a backdrop and tried to work out a few poses. I really felt uncomfortable, and from that day on I had a lot more patience and understanding for the models when I put them in this situation. The same goes for my downline now. I like to personally try everything that I suggest to people so that I can have a good feeling for all the challenges they might encounter.

> **The best way to build is to choose an action that we can be passionate about, and the more passion we have the less resistance we will experience.**

This is also true in our personal lives. The more passion we bring to our relationships, the more excitement there will be and the energy will flow through us.

For me, the most important relationship in my life is with God. This is the basis on which I build everything, and it is here that I find the qualities that I like to express, when I am alone and when I am with others. We might have different bodies, but we are all created from the same essence, and this essence is forever around us, embracing us, permeating our very beings. If we are to find peace in our lives it will benefit us to act in harmony with this essence. Some call this essence God, others by some other name. If we are to live as an extension of our Creator, then we should love in the same way, with the same unconditional love, loving everyone and everything without separation of any kind. If we are all part of the same emotion, every time I hurt you, I am also hurting myself. Every time I deceive you, I deceive myself. As we are all one heart, everything I feel, you feel. As we grow in awareness and expand our consciousness we are able to know this in a more tangible way. We are connected to every person who makes a breakthrough of any kind because we all swim in the same ocean of love. And when someone suffers, we also are part of this suffering. The masters of this world are able to love both the fire and the garden with the same equanimity, because they know they are of the same essence.

When Charles Possick built his downline from the creative idea of marrying direct mail and network marketing, we all grew with him. When Ghandi showed the world the power of non-violence, we all felt this power with him, and as hundreds of thousands of people felt free, we tasted freedom. We cannot separate ourselves from the truth of this unity. We can forget it, we can remain unconscious to this knowing, but the truth still stays the truth. By ignoring something you are certainly able to diminish its hold over you, but you can't stop time by ignoring it. When you go to sleep you still wake up later.

> **Our most important relationship is the one we have with ourselves, and with our source of creation. Whatever feelings you have about yourself will be the same as those you have about others. When you trust yourself, you are able to trust others. When you have faith in your own divinity, you are able to experience this divinity in others.**

When my life appeared to fall apart, I questioned my faith. I asked many questions to God, but I couldn't hear any voice with answers, and my heart seemed unable to experience love. I would pray and feel disconnected. Whatever I tried did not feel good, and I lived in fear. I no longer trusted myself, so I was unable to trust others. I was obsessed with my problems, and I lived with a constant focus on myself as a victim. I had spent my life learning how to focus energy, so I was very good at playing the victim role.

As a photographer I would often shut out the world around me except for what I saw through a small opening in my camera. I became so good at blocking out the rest of the world that I would drive others nuts because I wouldn't hear them talking to me while I was focused on the limited world I saw through the viewfinder. So while I was focused on my role as a victim I wasn't seeing or experiencing the opportunities that were coming my way. New relationships with great potential came and went, and my heart was in pain because I wasn't allowing my love to flow. Because our natural condition is a loving one, when we are not loving, we feel pain. By staying consciously aware of where we source our love from, we are able to access this love, and when we are loving there is less fear, and where there is less fear there is usually less pain.

> **When we are able to love ourselves and embrace our darkness, we are then able to be with others in a compassionate way, because we are more likely to love them and be able to embrace their darkness as well.**

I have found that I have a great ability to attract into my life those people that mirror back to me a lot of myself. When I communicate with others in the business world, it has become easier for me to see myself in others. I have certain tendencies that if they were to go unchecked would look exactly like some of the qualities of people that I meet and am at odds with. I have a number of people in my downline that want great results, but don't really put in a lot of effort. There are some who complain about all the time they spend on the phone, there are others who don't like sending follow-up packs. I can identify with each one of these people because through their hearts I can feel my own. There were times in my networking career that I hated to talk to new people, and there were times that I hated to talk to my friends. Almost every objection they experience I have some experience of myself.

My relationship with them is also about my relationship to these issues, and as I clear up these issues it shows them that they can clear them up. As they see and feel my faith work, because they are a part of me, their faith gets stronger.

Just recently I got a fax from someone on my first level who had built a fairly strong business, and they were looking at other opportunities. Rather than get too upset, I aligned myself with their feelings and understood that they did not trust our current opportunity as much as I did. I am totally convinced that as they focus their energy on their new opportunity that they will disconnect even more from their present downline. As they get divided within their own hearts, this will reflect more and more in their lives. For a long time they were even in income with two other couples that were building businesses on my first level. There is one couple that has stayed completely focused on their Cell Tech business, while the other couple has also been looking at other opportunities. Now both of the couples that are looking at other opportunities feel, of course, that this does not interfere in any way with their current business. However the couple that has remained totally and singularly focused on Cell Tech now has a check twice that of the others.

I don't think that it was necessarily the actual action of signing up with another company that caused this, but rather the mindset that allowed the whole thing to come about.

> **Once there is a crack in the container that holds the love, it is an opening for the erosion of faith.**

I know about this because I have experienced this myself. So the relationship that each person had within themselves created an allowing of the focused energy to become dissipated.

I have heard many successful entrepreneurs state that it is not a good idea to put all your eggs in one basket, so I can appreciate that people can have different viewpoints, and different ways of going about things. But to me having a second networking business is like having two spouses. There are not many of us who can make an enduring success out of one primary relationship, much less two. I definitely believe in leaving a lot of space for each person to make their own conclusions, and what I am sharing here is my personal feelings and thoughts about what will lead to healthy, productive relationship. There are always exceptions, and I do acknowledge that.

> **Clear, focused attention has a lot of power.**

For me, I enjoy experiencing energy like this, when I receive it and when I am the one sharing it. Relationships grow closer when each person is able to be totally present for the other, and when we are fortunate enough to share moments like these with loved ones, our need of having more people in our life gets reduced. That is why so many new lovers like to be alone, because they experience the whole of creation with and through each other. When I am with my four kids, totally present, I don't wonder what it would be like to have more kids around. In that time it is as if they are my whole world. What happens is that the experience is so joyous that we seem to attract others into our energy field.

Imagine that you only have one person in your downline, which is something we have all experienced at one time, if only for a short while. If you were to completely focus all your love and attention on that relationship, completely nourish this other person and honor them 100 percent, (and this might mean leaving them a lot of space) chances are that the wonderful vibration of this relationship would attract others to you. At the same time, if you developed a frustrating relationship with this person, you would probably attract more of the same. By loving we attract more love. By being free and powerful ourselves we will attract free and powerful people into our lives.

> **As we all grow through the archetypal patterns of relationship, and as we learn more about ourselves in relation to each other, we make it easier for all those who follow. Networking, whether done as a business or for the simple joy of sharing, is a way to connect.**

All our cells are connected, all our thoughts are connected, all our feelings are connected within ourselves, and as my energy reaches out to embrace yours, we are connected.

Two people sharing a lot of intimate time together become a collective force. When your energy melts with someone to co-create a business or build a downline, everything appears magnified. I remember the feeling of having dozens of people all focused on sponsoring new people into Cell Tech, and how we were all connected through the process. Their success became mine, and I felt a part of their lives.

Daryl Kollman once said that the Cell Tech distributors were his arms and his legs. He was experiencing these people as an extension of himself. We are all an extension of Divine energy, and we are all connected to each other through our source. As one of us grows, the whole collective ocean of our consciousness expands, and we are able to experience this expansion. When all the strings of a guitar are strummed only the most trained ear can differentiate the sound of each individual string. Out of the whole symphony of thoughts created by humanity, some thoughts reach out more than others, but we are all part of this creation.

While I was going through the breakup of my marriage, I was experiencing what felt like massive pain to me, and I have come to understand that it wasn't just my pain I was experiencing, but the collective pain of all my brothers all over the world going through a similar situation. As I tried to convince my wife that there was a better way, I felt massive resistance, and I was experiencing the collective resisting energy of all the women everywhere who felt the need to start a new life and did not want to stay in their marriages.

As we experience our issues through our relationships, it is important to not think of yourself alone, and that sometimes what you feel is your connection to the total pool of energy in which you live.

> **If you learn to rejoice in the success of your friends rather than be envious, you will be acknowledging your own capacity for success.**

> **There exists an enormous reservoir of love out of which we were all created and to which we are able to return and drink at will when we remember the path.**

It is from being in this pool that we know that the love is unlimited, that it is always there for us, and that the more we drink from it the more we add to it. This is the source of all abundance of any sort, and the spiritual laws that govern one aspect of our lives work in all the other aspects as well.

Cell Tech has, as its main product, a natural superfood called Alphanizomenon Flos Aquae or Super Blue Green® Algae. This is a fresh water algae that grows wild in the Upper Klamath Basin of Southern Oregon. The more one harvests this algae, the more it can reproduce. Thus this primordial food exists in nature and is maintained by the same spiritual law which was just mentioned. The more each one of us absorbs and shares the love from the universal pool of creation, the more this pool expands and the greater the amount of love there is.

When I started to eat the algae, I felt a sense of expansion from within myself. I felt connected to nature in a way that I had not felt consciously, and I understand now why this lake is capable of feeding so many thousands of people.

> **When someone or something is in a relationship that is harmonious with universal laws there is no limit to what can be accomplished.**

Divine energy is a totally inexhaustible source of nutrition for body, mind and soul and as long we collectively respect this, there will always be available what is needed.

If you learn to respect each person and things in your life as an aspect of the Divine, your relationships will flourish, and you will flourish. There is no limit to how many people you can touch with your love. Only conditional love has limits, but if you open yourself to experience unconditional love, you will also open yourself to unconditional growth. We have learned conditional love from other humans, because at no time does Divine energy come to us in a conditional manner. True spirit has no bounds, and knows no limits. One of the biggest gifts we can give ourselves and thus others is to share our love, and as we open our hearts, the hearts of all others will open. Global transformation starts with personal transformation, and when we are nourished with love we grow fast and truthfully. We can then share this with others and all grow together.

> **Not only is our relationship with ourselves and others of vital importance if we want to grow a big business, but our relationship to the earth and all this implies plays a key part in our growth process.**

One of the things that drew me to Cell Tech was that I met so many people who were able to guide me with integrity about issues concerning global stewardship.

I have a lot of respect for the way the company pays attention to things that I had not thought a lot about. When I attended company functions, I was able to hear speakers like Bernard Veserly, Jim Carpenter and Daryl Kollman talk about our planet and help me grow in awareness about things that were happening that I had chosen to ignore. I have come to accept that our lives are determined as much by what we choose to do as what we choose not to do. By ignoring taking certain action steps in my personal life concerning the well being of our planet, I was not living in harmony with the spiritual laws I so respect. By not living in harmony with these laws I was stunting my own growth, and my relationship with our earth was not nearly as meaningful as it could be. As I paid more attention to what was going on with the earth, I realized that the more responsibility I assumed about caring for our planet, the more I felt nourished by it. This allows me to feel good about accepting money for sharing something that the earth shares with me, and by paying more respect to my relationship with the earth, I feel more connected to my Creator.

> **When I feel more connected to my Creator, the quality of my whole life improves, as does the efficiency with which I do business.**

Chapter Nine

Tools for Action

How does one go about building a large network, and what are the tools that one uses to create maximum efficiency? As in everything else, I believe that the way to have a rich and rewarding life is to do everything we do in life with free flowing passion about what we are doing.

When actions come from our heart they are in harmony with who we are and who we want to be and because they come from a good energy they also create a positive energy. When you love what you are doing it is easier to detach from the results because the action itself is rewarding.

When I reflect on what worked for me in building my business to many thousands of people in less than a year and a half, there are many thoughts that come to my mind. I have a great upline, I have a great downline, I had the opportunity of some incredibly wonderful recruiting tools, I have the backing of a powerful company vision and I have what I believe to be the world's best nutritional food. But then, everybody in Cell Tech has the same tools available to them. It's true, that there is the variable of the upline, and certainly the downline, and many people would express the opinion that it was also that I had great lists. All of this is true, but before these lists were bought, others could have bought them. It is too easy to always look at some outside element, but what really makes the difference?

When two pitchers throw a baseball, they both throw the same ball, so why is one sometimes so much more effective than another. There are other companies that have access to the same algae as Cell Tech's.

For me, what makes the difference is the quality of passion and integrity that exists during the executing of each action. When there is a lot of love present with each moment, this love will help create a very positive outcome. I believe that the difference is on the inside. When there is a window of opportunity, some people just jump ahead and don't let fear stop them. They take action instead of creating excuses. And this is what I did. I surrendered to the love, and let the love carry me to create momentum. Because I love the entire Cell Tech experience so deeply, I was able to expand my entire being.

I don't think it is possible to create a network bigger than ourselves. We all start with the same action, when we sign up, but what differs is the level of commitment, and this is usually directly proportionate to the amount of love we feel. As my love grew, so did my passion, and the more that I learned about Cell Tech and the more I ate of the algae, the more my love grew, and along with this came passion, dedication, commitment and all the fuel that comes from a full heart.

So my favorite tool is love, and all that love brings. What the love does is connect me to everything. I had tried using the same abilities in other companies before, but never with such outstanding results, because my heart was not in harmony with their visions, thus my love did not flow so easily. When my love is blocked I usually encounter some form of resistance, and in building my Cell Tech business I felt really open, and all the actions were mostly fun. When we have a really strong why, the how just seems to take care of itself.

Let me use this philosophy to explain how I would choose a tool, or a path of action. I am someone who absolutely loved recruiting through the cold market, so it worked for me. I am someone who has a passion for the warm market, so that also worked for me. *I have found that I am less effective with action steps that I don't love, so what do I do? I hire someone to do it who loves it.* That way, my business is done in a loving way, even if it's not me personally.

One of the things that I really value highly is *time freedom*, so I always try to delegate. Isn't the nature of our business to create duplication? While I am enjoying writing this article there are people everywhere recruiting new people into our business. And what are the tools being used? I hope they are all derived from love–tools such as passion, commitment, integrity, being totally present in each moment, caring more about the other person than ourselves, helping others feel connected and part of our family–in short, unconditional love. Isn't this what we all want? I believe that if you want something, give it away, or said differently, be the person you want to recruit.

Once you have written out a purpose statement and have deeply understood why you are doing something, it becomes easier to choose tools that are in harmony with your purpose.

> **When you take actions that are fun for you and that you feel good about, the results are usually better.**

Take, as example, those who really loves going to a gym and working out. They go every day for a few hours, and are always in a good mood when they are there. Other people in the club recognize their well being and sense of joy and find them very charismatic. Their purpose in life is to help others find optimum health, physically, emotionally and spiritually. One of their action steps is to accomplish this by sharing the Cell Tech opportunity.

One day they make up a basket full of tapes to leave in a very conspicuous place. The basket is very well presented. A really nice photo of them, happy and in vibrant health, is on the front and there is a short text inviting people that are interested in maximizing their fitness program to take a free tape. There is also a small box asking people to leave their name and phone number, if they are interested, to participate in winning a free prize (this is for generating leads). Every day a person goes to the club, replenishes the basket, possibly putting fresh flowers with it. The little basket radiates love and light, joy and well being, and over the next few weeks, the little basket furnishes many new clients and leads. A small community within the club community starts to build, and people exchange stories about the positive results.

One day while on a conference call a person shares with the group that the little tape basket in her club has helped her make executive and create some nice momentum with her business. Someone hears this and decides that he will try this idea because it has worked so well. However, he is 40 pounds overweight, is a real couch potato and doesn't even belong to a health club. But he is a good salesman, and convinces a local club to let him put a basket there. Unfortunately the club is a 20 minute drive from where he lives and not in the direction he usually goes, for he rarely gets out of the house (this is why he likes a home based business) except when he goes to the local sports bar where he goes to watch sports on TV. However, every week or so he goes by the gym to see what is going on.

Can you imagine him having the same success as those who are having a lot of enjoyment with the same action. I would suggest to this gentleman that he try a tape in his local sports bar instead, because it fits more with his lifestyle.

> **Have you ever watched the kind of person who is always busy and yet never seems to get a lot done, and then watch a person with purpose accomplish massive results in a short amount of time?**

I prefer quality to quantity, and I believe that quality action is a lot more efficient. Just as I believe that quality people are easier to work with than large amounts of people who do little. That is why it is said that 80% of the work is done by 20% of the people. I have never really looked specifically, but I am quite sure that 80% of my line was built by less than 10% of my people. I have also come to learn that the success of these people was due to the fact that they all did a lot of little things rather than one extraordinary thing. When I built my business every day I would do many small things that at the end of the day amounted to a lot, and I repeated this daily over and over again. I truly believe that a lot of people could have done what I did. That is why it is said that in network marketing there are a lot of ordinary people making extraordinary income.

Just like many others there were moments when I had some fear, but I never let the fear hold me back.

Instead, I would always change my focus to something more positive. Every one in Cell Tech had the same tools to work with that I did. The lists that were passed down to me were available to others, the tapes that I sent out, anyone could have bought, and the information packets were something that each of us could have used. Many people just simply waited because they wanted to see if it worked for others first.

> **Not every window of opportunity stays open forever. There are red lights and green lights in our world, and if you don't move during the green light, you will find yourself waiting during the next red light.**

In our lives the windows of opportunity do not always operate with the same regularity as traffic lights, so when it is time to move we have to be aware that the window is open and we must take the action steps that are necessary. If vision is to become reality then thought must be turned into action. Unless a whole lot of people took action and actually created a laptop computer out of the thought processes that conceived it, I would not be able to write this book on this machine. If it was still just a thought in someone's mind I would have to use a different tool to express myself. No building tool has great value unless you use it. The tape basket as an idea does not carry the same force as the manifestation and use of the basket. When love and passion are added into the equation the same tool becomes a much more powerful possibility.

Let us return to the baseball for a minute. In the hands of the proper person this tool can become a vehicle for enormous personal growth and transformation. Not too many years ago a young pitcher on the Los Angeles Dodgers by the name of Orel Hershiser got into "the zone," as athletes call it. Inning after inning he stayed concentrated and focused and ended up breaking the record for most consecutive innings pitched without giving up a run. He then went on to lead his team to a world championship. During this run to become a world champion there were many moments where the other teams had small windows of opportunity, but in these moments Orel would always bear down and come up with a great pitch. He wasn't a lot better than anyone on the field, but the small difference that was there accumulated to make a big difference in the end. One thing that happened is that his ability to stay focused leveraged out into the rest of the team. As the team got through each level of playoffs, each individual member started to believe more and more that a world championship was really possible. As Orel remained a dominating force with his ability to throw a baseball, his and their futures changed dramatically. Orel Hershiser became a world champion and a millionaire because of his ability to use the baseball as an effective tool. Now ever since I was a boy this tool was available to me to build a life in baseball if I so desired, but even though I loved baseball I never developed my abilities the way he did. It wasn't one pitch that made the events that transpired so extraordinary, but rather the thousands upon thousands of pitches that he had thrown during his life.

There wasn't one phone call that built my business, but thousands of phone calls. Persistence and consistence were the keys, and actually taking action rather than thinking about the possibilities.

It is well known that in network marketing sometimes people get lucky and sign up one person who builds their whole business for them, but I'm convinced that if you really analyzed the event you would see that there were a lot of small and seemingly inconsequential things that happened to lead up to that event, and that if just one of these smaller things had not happened then the larger picture would not have unfolded. It is not always the one big massive thing that happens in our lives that changes everything.

During the break-up of my marriage my wife told me that she had met someone else and that it totally surprised her, and that it felt like her heart stopped. For a long time I thought about this moment and came to realize that the reason this happened was because of enough accumulated moments of disconnection between us that we didn't even consciously notice. There were probably countless windows of opportunity that we were offered that we didn't notice to save our marriage, but it felt easier to ignore them. That is why not doing something can alter your life as radically as doing something different.

> **Choosing to take action or not take action can both create powerful outcomes.**

If Ghandi had chosen to not choose non-violence as a tool of freedom, there would have been a totally different outcome and a different message received by everyone. Non-violence became a powerful tool of liberation because he chose to use it and to take action. There was no one monumental action that freed India, but the consistence and persistence of steadfastly refusing to give up his dream.

One of the challenges people have when choosing a tool to build their business is that sometimes they choose a tool because it worked for someone and not because they really love it themselves.

So many people are used to doing things that they don't love just to put food on the table, and so used to working for others and doing what they are told to do, that when they are free to build their own business and choose to do something they love, they don't even recognize that this freedom exists. Most people I know that make a living doing something they love would absolutely refuse to make a living doing something else. It is not the money that drives them but the love of what they are doing.

I don't think that through all his teen-age years Orel Hershiser thought very much about how rich he would become because of his ability to throw a baseball, but I bet in his mind's eye and in his heart he had thrown hundreds of

pitches that won a world series. He had a passion for playing baseball, and the passion is what drove him to his greatness.

Once we discover our purpose, the next step is to determine what action steps we can take that are in alignment
with this purpose and that are things that we enjoy doing.
That is why during my seminars I start the process by having
people write out their talents and their qualities, because
when it comes time to choose action, I can help them choose
action steps that will be fun for them. If I know someone has
a passion for skiing I will help them find action steps that are
based on this passion, and if someone else tells me they have
a passion for cooking I am not going to suggest to them that
they try to sponsor people on ski lifts.

> **When people choose action steps that feel
> good they usually will do them joyously
> and they will have more fluidity.**

Fluid and joyous action usually produces better results.
Peoples hobbies and talents are usually good indicators of
where they like to play, and the more people can feel like
work is play, the more successful people will be.

As I am writing this I am at Cell Tech's winter carnival
in Costa Rica with two of my children, Justin and Tara. Each
year a group of us get together to have a holiday together.
Every August we also have a big gathering we call the
August Celebration. The co-founders call us "The
Celebration Company." Each day here is a mixture of work-
shops, lectures and just playing together. For a lot of us, this
is how we work. There is no law that says work should not
be fun.

One of the joys of networking is that there are so many
different ways to express ourselves, doing things that we
love, that actually build our businesses. I heard a number of
people sharing that they signed people up on the airplane on

the way here. I love the idea that while taking a holiday for two weeks I could actually do more to increase my business than by staying home. Maybe one of those people who got signed on a plane will become the biggest builder in the organization.

Every time you choose an action that is done in a joyful manner, there is a vibration that accompanies this action that adds more power to it. Think of how you accept things in your own life. Last night I ate with a friend in a restaurant and the waiter had such a wonderful, happy manner about him that it made eating there a joyous occasion. I would go back there just because I enjoyed his energy so much. He could have sold me anything. In the same manner, when you go to a restaurant with poor service, no matter how good the food is, if the experience is not fun you probably won't return.

When I present the Cell Tech opportunity to people I am so full of energy, optimism, and a sense of well-being that people don't want to resist my offer. They can sense my love and passion and my commitment. *Whatever tool I use is infused with this positive power.* Because there is no doubt in my being about the validity of what I am doing, I believe that I could sponsor someone using a newspaper if I had to. I would just pick up a paper and find tons of things that would illustrate the magnificence of my opportunity. So it's not the tool that counts so much as what is in your heart. Positive energy attracts positive energy, and as we learn more about energy fields, we realize that when we meet someone there is a lot of unspoken communication going on.

One time I walked into a cage with a large puma, who seemed very quiet and friendly. At one point the cat put his front paws on my shoulders from behind. I felt OK, and was not experiencing any fear at that time. However, one of his claws got caught in the clasp of a leather necklace I wear around my neck, and I got a little nervous. Because the person with me couldn't get the claw unstuck I felt my fear rising, and as my fear rose the puma started this rather loud growl. For a moment I was really scared and in this moment the cat almost howled. I had said nothing but his energy knew mine right away.

When we meet someone a lot of unspoken communication happens on subtle energy fields. We know when we meet a loving person, and when we are loving people ourselves we feel a compatibility immediately. Watch kids get together that don't know each other on the first day of school, and undoubtedly all the trouble makers will gravitate towards each other. Watch adults do the same thing. Because we have an inner sense that talks to us, when we are in touch with ourselves we are able to use these powers of discernment in a positive way.

I believe that we have the same sense ability concerning an object. When we eat food that has been prepared in a loving way, even if we are not consciously aware as we eat it, I believe it digests better. So if you sent a prospecting tape or any other tool to a prospective customer, internally this person will have a reaction that is sometimes more important than the external one. Our unconscious responses are powerful because they guide us in a way that often we are not consciously aware of, and we do things without really knowing why. If one day someone decides to send bulk mail in a less impersonal way, addressing the envelope with lovingly careful handwriting, I think people will have a harder time throwing the envelope away still unread.

Chapter 10

Communication

I feel that it would be very hard today to build a network and maintain it without the use of the telephone. There are, of course, exceptions, but of all the current technologies available to us today, for me, the one I use to the most advantage is the telephone. For people who hate the telephone, this can create some major challenges if they want to work in our business; and I know some people who have to face this challenge. They prefer one-on-one meetings or large gatherings, but in my case, I use the phone and I use it a lot.

There has been an amazing amount of progress in the last decade around the telephone and we have all been able to benefit, and I think that in the future we will see even more capabilities developed that today we are not aware of. Fiber optics have replaced the old telephone cables. We can direct dial all over the world now, and people are even starting to speak through their computers. Video phones and video conferencing are becoming popular, and I can only imagine that in the not too distant future it will be common to talk to people while we see them on our televisions. Many U.S. homes have a home based business of some sort today, and more and more homes are equipped with multiple phone lines, fax machines and copiers. As we reach the year 2000, the ways people communicate and share ideas are in a continual state of change and transformation, just as we are.

I learned so much about myself and others through developing skills for the telephone and these skills have served me to be a better communicator.

When you learn to talk to people on the phone and truly connect with them, face to face becomes much easier. I have noticed that many shy people have an easier time building relationships on the phone because they feel intimidated with a face to face encounter; and once they have learned to connect with others through the safety of the phone, they then have more confidence when meeting with people in the flesh. Once you have tasted success in one part of your life, it becomes easier to experience success in other areas because you know the taste of success.

I took a tennis lesson one time and all the pro had me do was try to hit the ball in the sweet spot of the racquet, not caring where it went. Once I had the feeling of the sweet spot, I would call out "one," and if the shot was not truly in the sweet spot, I would call out "two," or "three," depending on how far off I was. The result of where the ball went was of no importance; so even if I hit the fence, instead of feeling bad, I would joyfully shout, "one," as if I had just hit a great winner. Before this lesson I would feel bad when I missed a shot, and now I was feeling good, even if I missed, because I had hit the ball well. The more times I hit the forehand with a "one," the better I felt. And then when I switched to trying backhands and volleys, it seemed that I immediately started hitting the ball in the sweet spot, just as I had gradually learned to do with the forehand. The success of the forehand was immediately applicable to the rest of my game. So one success may give birth to many others.

When I first started on the phone, I would spend a lot of time trying to impress people with how much I knew. I would send a tape to people and when they called for information I would start a five minute monologue which basically repeated everything that was on the tape. One day, early on in my telephone career, I got to the point where I asked which of the two specials I had mentioned would they like, and there was no answer because they had hung up the phone–so I changed my tactic. I shifted into frequently asking questions, because that way I knew I was talking with someone. I learned there is a big difference between talking to someone or at someone, and talking with someone. As I continued to ask questions I realized that my results increased, and I not only signed more people but I learned more about them so it became a lot easier to stay connected with them and help them get bonded to the product.

> **So idea number one is to not let your agenda interfere with communication. In other words, find out what they want and try not to let what you want direct the course of events.**

Pay close attention to what they say, and don't use your listening time to prepare your response. Learn to trust that you will have an adequate response without deciding ahead of time what it will be.

One of the challenges I am having in writing this book is that I can never remember if I have already written about something or not. Since I lead seminars every weekend and speak for two hours Friday, and eight hours Saturday plus do conference calls and my own phone calls, everytime I sit to write it is a challenge to remember whether I have already written or just spoken about something. When I thought about this, I decided to just plunge ahead and continue to write from a stream of consciousness because that is how I express myself the best, and if I end up repeating ideas, I figure it's because they are important to me. Often in my life I heard things literally dozens of times before I really got the

idea, and so I am going to plunge forward and not try to filter what comes when I am in the mood to write.

This brings me directly to another idea I want to share. I
feel that it is important to do things when they feel right for
you. I am fortunately in a position now where I don't have to
write this book. I am doing it because I want to.
Consequently I can afford the luxury of writing only when I
am inspired to. And this is also now how I do my phone
work. Unless I am in the mood to talk, I usually don't initiate phone calls, but I almost always answer my phone if I am
not already talking to someone. My intent now is to restore
balance and harmony into my life, to diversify some of my
action so that I produce results in different areas of my life.
Yet when I built my network I came from a different
approach. I wanted to "create a storm" as my friend Gilles
Arbour calls it, so I was on the phone sometimes fifteen
hours or more a day. Although there were times when I struggled, most of the time I was having a ball. Because I wanted
to build with a lot of momentum, because there was a window of opportunity at that time I wanted to take advantage
of, because I was so fed up with being in pain that I wanted
to follow the advice of my friend Martine, and "turn that
pain into a passion," I loved being that busy and I would do
it all over again gladly. If the opportunity came again to
spend all that time and be able to sign as many people as I
did, I would do it all over again, although this time I would
simply hire more help to assist with all the daily chores, letters, welcome kits, info packs, etc.

Many of my downline were saying they thought it was
great that I was getting so much success but that they didn't
feel that they wanted to invest all the time that I did. I know
that most of them are kicking themselves now, wishing that
they had taken a bit more time because the success lasts a lot
longer than the time I invested. Now they are spending a lot
more time than I am and I have a lot more freedom, and my
check will last for years. As in all domains of our life, we
have choices and I chose to build fast but that does not mean

that everyone should do the same. In fact, in many cases, if people can afford the time to build slowly and steadily, I would recommend it.

> **The important thing is to be happy with your choice.**

What I experience is that people do the actions which will create slow growth and are unhappy that they aren't making the big checks quickly. This is what doesn't make sense. Expectation can and almost always will create unhappiness. We need to be able to take an action, enjoy the doing, and then let go and not get tied to the outcome. I am constantly amazed at how many people want great results with no effort. I believe that enlightened masters are capable of entering into this kind of energy flow, but they have gotten there by a deep commitment to the spiritual disciplines they learned and a lifetime of study. Most people that I know who enjoy success at some time have paid their dues. And when they haven't paid their dues, such as winning a lottery or receiving money through inheritance, I have seen people unable to cope with receiving this kind of abundance because they haven't developed the self worth to contain it.

I've taken a bit of a divergence here, because my intent when I started this chapter was to talk about phone skills, so let's get back to that.

When I was literally tied to the phone, there were times when I wanted to take a break, but didn't. This might appear to be a contradiction to what I said earlier about talking only when I wanted to, but different tasks are usually required at different stages of our lives. It is totally appropriate for a baby to stumble while they are learning to walk, but if I was to continue to stumble at my age, it might appear a bit ridiculous. If you watch some babies, they can grow very frustrated with falling, but most of them just smile, and get up and try again. For me, talking long hours on the phone when I built my business was like the baby learning to walk. Maybe I didn't always like it, but I knew if I wanted to have success this was a stage that I had to pass through, and I wanted to pass through it quickly, which I did. Once I know I have to do something, I accept it and do it as joyfully as I can.

Now, I travel every weekend to my Relay 2000 events, and people ask me all the time if it doesn't burn me out. Because I love to serve through trainings, (the way our company does trainings now is by sending the trainers to the different cities) travel is part of the package. So I made a conscious decision to enjoy the time spent traveling. I use the hour to the airport to either make phone calls, listen to tapes or music or learn a language or just think. Once I get to the airport I go into prospecting mode and see how many tapes I can hand out. While on the plane I do the same, and I read a lot (which I really enjoy) or I write or just take notes. I look at this as my alone time and I can do whatever I please. So instead of looking at the travel as a hassle, I experience it as a wonderful time. I also take my younger children with me and they get to travel and see other cities and make lots of new friends.

When I was on the phone and experiencing burnout, I would do many different things to change my energy. One of them, which I learned from Brian Biro at one of his seminars, was simply lift up my chin as far as I could and smile as wide as possible. It is impossible to feel bad when you do this exercise, and I would sense an immediate change within myself. Sometimes I would stand up and walk around to get some energy flowing through me, other times I would just go sit out in the sun and relax while I talked. I have a foot massage machine from Sharper Image that I keep under my desk, so sometimes I would turn this on, or I would use the massage pad a friend gave me that is in my super deluxe desk chair. I have a salt water tank in my office that I can gaze at while I talk, or I can look out the window to the beautiful

Sandia mountains. I have created a very comfortable and fun environment for myself in the room where I work, and I splurged on a really comfortable desk chair so I feel that I am at a command station of the Star Ship Enterprise. I wear comfortable clothes while I talk, so that I feel good. And I have pictures of my kids where I can see them along with quotes that inspire me. My computer screen is the extra large kind and in color so I don't strain my eyes so much. In other words, I like to spoil myself. I am not particularly attached to these things but I love having good, clean efficient tools with which to accomplish things. My phones are all high quality, as is my copier and fax machine. I have speaker phones and head sets so I can choose whatever I want to use. I have a small TV in my office with a tape deck, so that I can tune in to things while I am doing actions that don't require my maximum attention. If I am placed on hold I can always find something to do if I so please, or I can just sit and go inside myself. I have multiple lines so that if I am on one phone and need to get some information I have another line. My fax and computer are on independent lines as well, so I never have to wait or experience challenges that can't be immediately resolved that might necessitate their use. It took me some time to build up all this, but I made a serious effort to not procrastinate instigating these ideas. If one day I experienced serious discomfort because I didn't have what was needed, I would then act immediately and get it taken care of.

> **When something presents itself, *do it*, because you never know when the window of opportunity will present itself again.**

My teacher Sidi calls this *"being the son or daughter of your moment."* When someone recommends a book that gives me a yearning to read it, I try to order it immediately, otherwise I tend to forget, and when it comes to my mind to make a phone call I try to do it then. People always ask me how I get so much done, and this is the answer–I don't procrastinate.

When I am on the phone, I make a conscious effort to not have interruptions, and when they keep coming I try to look into the moment and feel if this is really the best time to be talking to this person. Often, people will draw out phone conversations, and just when it is appropriate to end the conversation another call will come in. When I am in a good space, I can have my whole day unfold like this, but if I am tired, or nervous, or impatient, it will seem as if every call comes in at the same time. While I am writing this I have had only two or three calls in the last hour, and I feel that when I am complete with this, that the phone calls will accelerate, unless I get preoccupied with something else. The universe has its own rhythm and it feels good when you are in harmony with it.

...It is now a few hours later and immediately upon finishing that sentence a friend stop by, the phone started ringing, and my kids came home from school. As soon as I focused on interruptions, that's exactly what I got.

There were a lot of times that I just did not feel like staying on the phone so much, so I would stop for awhile, take care of other office chores, and then literally find myself driven to get back and start phoning.

I remember talking to Pete Buntman about this and he told me the same thing happened to him. He got into this space where when he got off the phone it felt like withdrawal. But there were times that I simply had to force myself, and everytime this would happen and I would resist going back on the phone, I simply looked at the fact of what my life would look like in a few years if I didn't make the calls.

As I built my organization, there were many times I did things that I didn't love doing, but I knew that if I continued one day I would be able to relax and hire people to help me.

As my momentum increased, I sure felt a lot better, and even though there was stress, it was a lot less than the stress of worrying all the time what I was going to do with my life and how was I going to support my four kids. I knew that for every one hundred phone calls I was closer to my goal of financial freedom and farther away from the fear of not being able to support my family. Every step I took brought me closer to my destination and left behind all I didn't want.

Granted as we mature we can accomplish a lot without massive action, because we are human beings and not human doings, but at some stage of our life we seem to need to learn about the doing, even if it is to let it go.

> **The thing is that we don't have to ask for things to be easier, we can choose to be better and stronger and smarter ourselves.**

One of the challenges with Cell Tech is learning effective ways to educate people about how to eat the products. If we are to be successful we simply have to learn how to do that, and the only way this will get easier is for us to learn more effective and efficient ways to accomplish this. One of the best ways we have currently is to do a lot of follow-up phone calls, and the more we call the better results people have, the more they connect with the product, and the more our volumes grow.

These calls are time consuming and not often everybody's favorite thing. People are more excited about signing up a new distributor than taking care of their current customers. I felt this often in my photography business. New clients seemed to always get me excited and rejuvenated when in actual fact the older clients were the ones supporting me. I'm not saying it makes sense to think like this, just pointing out the reality.

So how do you develop great phone skills, once you have disciplined yourself to make the calls? Without a doubt, the most valuable tool on the phone is to be able to listen. My teacher always refers to something he calls the *adab*, or the *deep polite*. He always tells me that God loves the deep polite and to always be very polite. One of the most polite things you can do is honor people by listening to them. So many people in today's world do not find people willing to listen to them. As Big Al says, you want to get people to know you, like you and trust you. Once you take the time to listen to people they will share more and more with you, and they will give you all the windows of opportunity you need in order to connect with them.

Personally, one of the things that interferes with my listening is distraction. Even when I am face to face with someone, if something happens in my range of vision I literally have to fight to not leave eye contact, or if I hear some other voices my attention might turn there. Another really big challenge for me is that people seem to take a long time to get to the point, and because it appears to me that I know where they are going with what they are saying, I either have a tendency to interrupt or let my attention wander. I am not proud of this, but it is my truth. These two things become magnified over the phone, so I have to take particular care to pay attention. A lot of times while I am in my office, if I am in a less than engrossing conversation, I have to resist not doing something else while I am talking, like straighten my desk or work on the computer. In order to focus more clearly I will get up and move away from my desk and all the distractions there, but then I can no longer take notes. So sometimes I just turn my armchair away from my desk to look into my salt water tank or out the window to the mountains.

A lot of independent distributors for Cell Tech use conference calls to connect with others, and I am invited once or twice a week to talk on these calls, and it's usually in the evenings. I live a very full life, and I love the late hours of the evening when I am really by myself, when the calls stop and the kids are in bed. I also like to get up very early, so sleep is not something I do a lot of. Consequently, during quiet moments, I sometimes feel fatigue. A conference call, where I am listening to others talk, is one of those times, and I really have to be careful not to fall asleep. On a lot of these calls I talk a lot, so that keeps me awake, but most of my close friends, the ones I talk to after 10 pm, have known me to fall asleep during our conversations. What happens is I lie down on my bed or lean back in my really cozy leather chair at my desk, and just relax so much I drift off. So sometimes I have to get up and walk around to keep alert. I know some business people who will not sit in a comfortable chair for a business meeting because they want to stay totally alert. If the body relaxes too much, the mind can too easily follow.

Cell Tech is a healthy company in every sense of the word; privately owned and debt free, in business for over fifteen years. We are financially healthy; and when you go to a company gathering, the people are vibrantly healthy physically. Spiritually the people who are involved with Cell Tech feel they are making a difference with their lives and contributing to the world in a positive manner because of all the programs, such as the Network of Hope, the Cell Tech Solution, and the Algae Pond Team to just name a few. In another part of this book I will discuss these programs and share how Cell Tech and other companies are creating new paradigms in the business community. When people feel that their lives are worthwhile, they feel healthy spiritually and emotionally, and experience what it feels like to live a fulfilled life style. Many of the Double Diamonds in Cell Tech are financially free enough to really pursue their dreams. For some it might be music, for others it might be to help others attain what they have, but whatever it is, they are doing it because they want to and not because they have to.

During my seminars I started to include a Sunday morning exercise which ended up teaching me a lot. After my normal seminar many distributors would ask me if I would help them with a three way call to someone in their line. Most of these people were not in my downline, so I realized that if I started to do this it would take a lot of extra time, and I started seeking inside myself for a solution, because I wanted to help people, but I wanted to do it in a way that would honor my life as well as theirs.

My friend Ira Greene, another Relay 2000 trainer, used Sundays to teach phone skills, and many people had told me they found it to be very helpful. Ira would put people in small groups and they would practice their phone skills, and they would all help each other. This gave me the idea to actually call people on a speaker phone so that the whole room would actually be able to hear me talk to people and experience first hand how I did the business, so it would be more than theory, it would be true life experience. People would put their name in a basket, and when their name was drawn out, I would call into their downline, or upline if they wished, and help them with whatever challenge they were experiencing. After the person gave me a brief profile of the person I was to talk with, I would simply call them and start a conversation, always telling them they were on a speaker phone because if you want people to trust you, it serves to tell the truth. When you get someone fully engaged on the phone, they will forget that others are listening.

These calls were always very interesting, because I didn't know any of the people before and I didn't want someone else's interpretation of them to cloud my intuition. I had to pay very close attention to every nuance so that I could find a place where I could really connect with them. *During these calls I would have to block out the room and the other people and stay completely focused with the person on the telephone, and I learned that when I did this I heard them with a much deeper ear and felt them a lot stronger.* I took a lot for granted in other communications because I felt that there would always be other opportunities, but in this case I knew that I might never speak to these people again so I wanted to accomplish something worthwhile before hanging up.

This reinforces how valuable giving yourself deadlines can be. I learned from doing these calls that I could accomplish the same thing when I talked to people in my organization by really paying attention to them when I was with them, and that in the long run it would save both of us a lot of time.

I just returned from Costa Rica and the Winter Carnival, and had the wonderful experience of attending a short seminar with Carol McCall, who specializes in helping people learn the art of listening. One of the things I learned for myself is that it is OK to ask people who tend to talk a lot to shorten their communications so that you can stay focused. What happens is that when you honor people by really listening to them, it feels so good to them, that they tend to want to talk more and more. So I am starting to say things like, "I really understand where you are coming from, and I am working now on staying really present with people, and while I am learning this skill it would really help me if you could get to the point quickly so that I can stay completely focused with you."

Most people will truly appreciate your honesty, and it will also help them to learn to organize their thoughts and express themselves more efficiently, so it's a win win for everyone. To sum phone skills up briefly, as in so many other areas of our life, if we share ourselves in a loving way and stay totally present, we will experience better results.

Chapter Eleven

Sponsoring

O ne thing that I didn't learn right away is the difference between sponsoring and recruiting. It wasn't until I got to the point where I accepted that I wasn't really doing a good job with follow up, and wanted to deal with this issue, that I learned that most of my challenges came from the way I introduced people into the business. I was so concerned with getting people to sign up that there were loop holes in my integrity which I later came to regret. I tended to exaggerate the situation in order to convince people to try our products, and not only was it not necessary, I believe that it created many more problems.

Expectations are a source of disappointment, and I prefer to under commit and over perform, and it feels better to me. I was so excited when I started that I let my enthusiasm run wild, which can be positive, but looking back and being honest I would have to say that I did overdo it a bit. I made unnecessary promises that didn't honor anyone concerned, especially Cell Tech. When someone sends the product back unopened because it was more than they expected, it costs everyone involved to expend unnecessary energy. This brings no satisfaction to anyone, least of all the customer. So I have stopped using the money back guarantee as a strong sales point, and now when I mention it I also tell people that they shouldn't start if the money back guarantee is what is convincing them. The product works well when people believe in it and in a new process that can bring better health and well being to their life.

We all have love inside of us, even though there are some of us who have challenges in feeling and expressing this love. When this love is blocked, we are the ones who feel the pain as well as those we hold back the love from.

When we truly sponsor someone, we offer this love as part of a support system, while recruiting someone usually means enticing them into your program without the benefits of the support system.

I learned a lot about this in going through the separation with Nathalie. My friend Kathleen Loeks suggested that what would be best is that if the love that took us into the relationship could continue to carry us, and to be truthful I feel Nathalie was probably more capable of this than I was. I allowed my ego to interfere so much and my love was so blocked, the pain was immense and rendered me totally dysfunctional. She was able to love me in a new way, but not only was I unable to do the same, I was unable to receive the love in this way. I just couldn't adjust at the time and see the wisdom of it all. As I have said before, I still don't advocate breaking up marriages especially where children are involved, but I know that I could have managed the situation with more grace and dignity if the little boy in me hadn't screamed so loud with all the abandonment issues I experienced. I am grateful for the man I have become, and there is a certain sadness in my heart that I couldn't have honored Nathalie more by accepting the situation with more integrity.

What does this have to do with sponsoring? I think that the principle is the same. What happened with Nathalie was that when I held back the love, there was no support system offered by me for her to help her in her transformation. The fact that there wasn't any support was an important part of her process, but I'm talking about me here. I'm suggesting that when you hold back the love, you deny the other person and yourself a true connection, and your agenda starts to supersede over theirs, and this is not a noble way to honor people.

> **When we bring a new person into our life and into our business we have to accept the personal responsibility to ourselves to be the best we can be.**

I am not saying we need to baby-sit anyone, I am saying that we owe it to ourselves to keep all channels of communication open, and to allow ourselves to be open in our expression. If we hold back a part of ourselves we are not being truly present, and if we are not fully present there are too many gaps where misunderstandings occur.

When we accept to fully sponsor someone, then we have accepted the responsibility of educating them in the use of our products and sometimes this can take months. There are many companies where this isn't really important, such as when someone uses a long distance service. You don't have to spend too much time educating people how to use a phone companies service, the company usually explains it all to them, and the only time where you might have continued connections is if you are teaching them how to do the business.

Basically when I did a networking phone opportunity I had a lot less responsibility and commitment towards the people that got involved, but I had a very low level of satisfaction in terms of feeling fulfilled. I didn't feel I had an impact in people's lives like I feel I have now, and my soul didn't resonate the way it does these days.

> **Right livelihood is something that can be totally transformational in our search for inner excellence, and our relationship with our work is as vital as our relationship with our spouses.**

Depending on our level of commitment and involvement with either, we can feel more or less fulfilled.

When Nathalie wanted to leave she expressed that the life she shared with me did not fulfill her, and I felt that one of the reasons was that her attention was focused outside.

I have always felt totally fulfilled in relation to my children, and the reason is that I fully invest my heart with them. I have never felt that I had to sacrifice anything for my kids, they have been a constant plus in my life, always giving me a wonderful feeling which adds immeasurably to my existence.

When I sold long distance rates to people I was jazzed because I liked the idea of financial freedom, but I couldn't get too passionate about selling low phone rates. So what held me back in the phone opportunity was that I wasn't fully committed to all of the experience, and you can't really offer to someone what you are not feeling yourself. Someone's higher self is going to know when you're higher self is not fully engaged.

When I found Cell Tech I got engaged one hundred percent, and everyone I met could feel it. When you meet couples that are deeply connected and totally engaged it is very charismatic. It often makes people feel that they would like to have an expression of love like this in their life. And when people sense you are fully engaged and passionate about every aspect of your work, they feel the same way.

I saw a T-shirt in Albuquerque airport last Sunday while waiting for my suitcase that said, "The most valuable possession you can own is an open heart. The most power-ful weapon you can be is an instrument of peace."–Carlos Santana.

Cell Tech has opened my heart and helped me feel I am an instrument of peace, and because of the gift of networking I can offer this to others. If I no longer feel that Cell Tech offers me this full expression of myself, I will move on elsewhere, because now that I have tasted what it is like to be fully engaged I don't think I could settle for less.

> **I feel that there is a divine presence which is the source of absolutely everything, and now I can see that this same force exists in everything, and I want to exist in a place where this presence which permeates all is obvious to all.**

By opening our hearts and letting the love flow freely, we are in constant communication with this divine energy, and this energy supports not only the individual but the whole world. Just like the ocean exists in every drop that makes up the ocean, the Divine exists in every heart that makes up our world. Love knows no limits and through knowing love we can taste the Divine, because once we have the experience of accepting there are things that have no limits, such as love, then we can make the step to accept other things greater than ourselves. We don't need anymore to be limited by our rational minds, but can reach knowledge by way of the heart and through the knowing of the heart, which is the path of the great mystics.

This feeling of completeness creates a joyful feeling of exhilaration, and when action springs forth from this condition it is usually very productive. When I first started sharing the products I focused a lot on how it had saved my life, so I drew to me people similar to myself, and now that I am in a more joyous state, I seem to draw happier people to me. What I desire now is people who have not lost their yearning for enlightenment, and who want to make a difference in the world. There are thousands of these people and I see them everywhere, and now I feel that it is appropriate that I draw them into my life because I have understood what it means to really sponsor someone, and I can be the kind of sponsor that they would consent to work with.

I look deeper now when I enter into a networking relationship with people, and if I feel any resistance I try to team them up with someone else on my first level, because I have decided that I want my time to be spent with people that have open hearts, because these people seem to be more connected to the source of true power. I am attracted now to the kind of person who wants to learn so that they can do things for themselves, who want to truly co-create rather than have you do it for them. I still love helping people and am committed to always doing this, and I have come to the realization that the more I help strong people the more total lives get touched.

One of the biggest fears I encountered in the people I talked with was that of sharing a networking opportunity with someone that was making more money than they were. They had no resistance to sharing with those making less, but had genuine fears about going to successful people with their opportunity. So many great ideas are brought into fruition by people who share their dream with powerful personalities.

If I write a great movie script it is doubtful that a local taxi driver is going to know how to raise the money to produce my script. I did say doubtful, not impossible. Many successful people find it very fulfilling to be able to help others still struggling, and if you don't have the courage to walk through your fear you are depriving them of this opportunity. We all have fears, but if you are passionate enough you can go through the fear and experience what is waiting

on the other side. It is the passion that will allow you this
grace.

> **Once you have accepted the responsibility
> of sponsoring someone, you now get to see
> how good you are at treating others as you
> would like to be treated.**

*How much patience do you have, how much under-
standing* to go over and over all those baby steps with everyone to ensure they understand to put this bottle in the ice box
and that one out of it, and eat one of this and two of that, and
tolerate all those questions that are so easily answered if they
would just read the 88 page deluxe color brochure you sent
and watch the video, and listen to that extra tape on the way
to work? I know how hard it is to understand why everyone
isn't as committed as you are, because if they only knew
what you knew, their life would be so much better, wouldn't
it? It is sometimes truly amazing that we all think so different yet how alike we really are. I have learned to be grateful
for these differences because it is from them that we learn.

*As we reach to embrace the Divine in all that we do,
than our experiences in the Divine begins, and this is the
journey that has no end and knows no limit. When you live
each moment in its fullness, not asking about or expecting
any particular outcome, totally committed with all of your
being to experience everything in its fullest potential, then
you have the opportunity to experience the true mystery of
life.*

Chapter Twelve

Windows of Opportunity

I am always amazed that even as I improve my ability to walk in awareness, I still miss a large number of opportunities, either because I am not prepared or because I simply don't recognize the opportunity until it has gone by. One of the biggest changes in my life and one that has brought me what feels like immense personal growth is that when things happen now that I react to with hurt feelings, before I act, or react, from these feelings, I ask myself a question. That question is simply, "Where is the opportunity?" By asking this question I take a moment to reflect so that I don't take things personally that weren't intended to affect me as such, and when they were, I have some time to create a more productive response. I don't remember where I heard about something called *the gap*, but the gap is the moment that exists just after someone finishes talking and before you start your response. This moment, when trusted, is always full of opportunities, and during this time, as you grow in awareness and feel relaxed within it, you will realize that you always have a number of responses to choose from. Most people start formulating their response to people before the other person even completes their phrase, I do this all the time, but when I wait patiently for them to finish and then sit comfortably in the gap, I realize that I have a lot of responses to choose from, or a lot more opportunities available to create my response from. The more I trust, the more creative this moment can become.

It took me a long time to realize that relationships were really about opportunities, because for a long time I experienced them more as an obligation. By this simple, but not easy, shift in attitude I feel I am more prepared now to co-create with another person rather than direct things to go in a manner that works for me. Part of my dysfunction was always worrying too much about the other person, and frequently slipping out of integrity in order to give responses that would work for them and get them to love me. This denies both of us the opportunity to explore what it would feel like to exist in a relationship where truth was more important than temporary satisfaction or false flattery. When we sweep enough dust that we want to hide under the rug, sooner or later the mound becomes evident and we trip over it.

> **The greater the challenge that we encounter, the greater the opportunity exists to find out who we are.**

When Nathalie felt drawn to new experiences, as painful as it was, there was also the seeds of many different opportunities. I could have done what I had always done in the past, which was to find solace in the arms of another woman, or in drugs of some sort. This time I was so depressed that women or drugs didn't even excite me, so it wasn't my great discipline or wisdom or integrity that saved me, but a higher power. Something inside me screamed so loud that I couldn't ignore it, and this voice suggested that if I kept on doing things the way I had always done them, that I would keep on getting the same thing over and over again.

My friend, Martine, the Shaman, told me that in my family lineage the men had always had this kind of trial, and that no one had successfully resolved it, so it was passed on down to me, and if I chose not to deal with it, my children would get this pattern. Now those are frightening words to me, because the last thing I could accept at this point was to be responsible for sending any pain like this down to my kids, so instead I took this opportunity to resolve this in a more productive manner.

> **Every moment of out lives we have a choice, and the choice is about how much love we are willing to open to and how much love we are willing to share. We are given this choice over and over and over, and we will still always have this choice as long as we are alive.**

Marianne Williamson, whose teachings are inspired from the *Course of Miracles*, speaks and writes about how everything either comes from love or from fear. Fear is such a negative, low vibration, and the more fear you allow in your life, the more fear you attract. Next time you have a choice that you are aware of, ask yourself which of the choices or options you are experiencing would be the one that would allow the most love in that moment, and then make that choice and watch how it feels.

Think for a minute about responsibility. We always have the choice to accept personal responsibility for the results in our life, both good and bad. Frequently, we all love to give ourselves a pat on the back when we accomplish something that we are proud of, but if we get a result that doesn't please us, if you are like me, you might look to some outside cause as to why something didn't go the way you expected. This was the big battle for me with the change of my marital status. I spent a long time blaming Nathalie for everything that had happened, and was determined to keep my victim status, no matter what.

Ava, one of the therapists, asked me once if Nathalie appreciated all the free therapy she was getting because I spent my whole hour analyzing her. I don't know when the shift occurred exactly, but I am now ready to acknowledge my part and the responsibility I had in creating the final result. Many times the idea of accepting that I consciously did something that goes against my apparent ideals and values is so hard to accept, that I stay in denial and let myself be directed unconsciously instead. A few years ago I was able to state, rather proudly I might add, that I had nothing to do with her decision to divorce, that I was against divorce, and that I was just surrendering to her will. A friend had told me that he thought I had the longest bull ride he had ever seen. Yet there must be some part of me that wanted this or I wouldn't have attracted it into my life. This is the stage where I am now, and I have a deep trust that I am very close to finally integrating everything in a conscious manner.

> **I want to know the whole truth of my being, I want to embrace both my light and darkness, I want to make my dark side conscious, so I am ready to accept this knowing.**

By writing this so openly I hope that the universe will know that this is my truth.

I just realized that I had a choice here, to expose this piece of unfinished business, or to hold it and not experience full disclosure. I teach in my seminar that when you stand up in front of others and share your purpose or your goals by speaking them out loud, this gives energy and power towards a more clear manifestation. So I chose to take this opportunity to express something that came to me, rather than withhold it.

When I started this chapter I was on a plane and had read an article by Jay Abraham, because I subscribe to his newsletter. I was struck by the word opportunity and decided to make this the subject of this chapter, but I had no conscious idea of what I would write, or how the chapter would turn out. I just took the opportunity from the word, and then again from the thought I had. What I am trying to point out here is that there are many opportunities to live life fully, completely in truth and with integrity, and with our hearts open and vulnerable. As I finish this thought, I now am free to go in the gap and see what comes next. In fact, I'm now sitting in Denver airport with about a forty minute wait and I think I'll go see if I can find someone with an energy I like and share a tape with them.

I just finished walking around a bit looking for an opportunity to share my opportunity with someone, and within minutes of creating this intention, a couple of kids came off the moving runway, full of energy, and then turned to wait for their mom and a third kid. All three kids were under ten, so I smiled at her and said, "Are these your kids?" And she answered, "Unfortunately, yes." Because she was feeling a bit hassled. Now I know what it's like to travel by yourself with kids, and it can try your patience. So I smiled, and gave her a tape and said, "Well, here's something you'll love, and it really is great for kids." She thanked me and took the tape. If she calls before I finish this book I'll be sure to let you know. One thing is for sure—I don't think she would have known how to call me if I hadn't gotten up and given her the tape.

I don't expect people to know about my opportunity if I don't share it with them.

As I'm sitting here writing I kind of keep looking up to see if there are other opportunities that I might be missing to share a tape, and realize that I am more interested in this opportunity to write than I am in sharing a tape; however there is a couple sitting behind me in their fifties or sixties, and while I was waiting and looking for someone, I did think about giving them a tape. They looked kind of tired, and not full of energy, and I thought that the algae could help them, but I didn't go up to them because from somewhere inside of me I felt resistance. They are an oriental couple, probably from the Pacific rim, and one of my goals this year is to share this opportunity with as many different cultures as I can, so I am always looking for an opportunity to connect with people that come from a different background or culture. And as I sit here, I can't get them out of my mind, and so I guess I'll go through my comfort zone and see what happens.

Well, I stood up to go give them a tape, but the husband is not sitting there now so I am going to wait and approach them together because I feel that it would be more polite. Actually, maybe this means he shouldn't be there when I offer the tape, so here I go.

Interesting. Here's what happened.

I walked up holding out the tape and said, "I would like to give you a present, it's a story about a fresh water algae that is similar to seaweed and I think you'll find it interesting," and she said, "No, I don't want it." And so I replied, "I think you and your husband will find this interesting," and she said to come back when her husband was there.

My internal dialogue is going something like this. My first instinct was that they had a fearful aura about them, and that's why I didn't go immediately to give the tape. Then I couldn't forget that they were really the first people I saw when I stood up to go give a tape, and they certainly fitted into my idea of cultural diversity. Then when she turned me down, I thought I should have listened to myself about waiting for the husband in the first place, and now I'm thinking that maybe they were there to illustrate all the different viewpoints about understanding what the opportunities are that surround us.

Because I was looking for someone to give a tape to, I was not holding in my consciousness the idea that the opportunity I saw them there for was not the opportunity that God intended to share with me at that moment.

The husband still has not returned, and I have lost a lot of my enthusiasm about giving them a tape, but I'm persistent and I think what I'll do is wait and see what opportunity presents itself when he is there. I am grateful for the moment because I learned from it that I still have a lot of work to do on learning to see and feel clearly.

Sitting right beside me is a gentleman about 45, I would guess, and he has a good start on a pot belly and would benefit from the enzymes, but I'm not drawn to him. A younger guy, with a good energy just came up and plugged in his computer just above mine, so we are kind of connected because we are sharing the same electrical plug, but he's wearing earphones as he's typing and I don't want to interrupt him.

Still no husband and they are calling my flight...
to be continued...

Well, this chapter is full of adventure. When I got up to go to the flight the husband was there, so I gave him the tape, which he accepted. Then when I got to the gate they had closed the door already. Fortunately I got them to open the door and let me on the plane. If I had missed this one, I would have missed my connection to Medford, and things would have been a bit more challenging. I think I need to pay a little more conscious attention to my priorities, because I don't want to miss planes unnecessarily.

What this is showing me is that it is a great gift to know that we can make conscious choices and don't have to live so unconsciously. When we live without conscious awareness, we suffer certain consequences without knowing how these moments arrived in our lives, similar to what happened in my marriage. If I had been more conscious I would have paid attention to Nathalie's growing dissatisfaction with her life, and undoubtedly mine as well. I was so caught up with *other stuff,* like day to day existence, that I missed some important things going on right around me. When you live a lot worrying about tomorrow, it means you are not truly present in the moment. And if you are not truly present in the moment, you are not living as fully as you could.

> **When we choose to live every moment in a loving manner, we are living as we were created.**

I believe in a God that created the universe and everything in it, and it doesn't matter to me how one calls or defines this energy. Call it unconditional love, the Divine, whatever you wish, but if you accept, as I do, the idea that we all come from a common heritage, that we are all connected through this heritage, then your well-being becomes as important as mine. If we dedicate every moment of our existence to being an extension of pure, unconditional love, we will feel more connected and thus be more connected. This means that every day, every moment we get to choose over and over again what opportunity we want to experience. I can not be responsible for your choices, and you are not responsible for mine, but if I witness someone that makes choices that continually keep them in a station of loving, like my teacher and guide, Sidi, then I am inspired to do the same.

When we accept the fact that we are personally responsible for what we create, that our life is a result of how we think, that we are free to choose how we want to think, and we are equally free to change our thoughts as we see what serves us and what doesn't, then we start walking with more awareness. In the last half hour my life was full of opportunities to make different choices, to take different actions, and the future will be as much a result of what I did as to what I didn't do. If I hadn't got up out of my chair and made this plane, this day would have certainly turned out differently. I wouldn't be sitting next to this gentleman who just shared with me that he is going to France this summer, (where I spent 25 years), with his wife and 19 year old son (I have a 20 year old, as you know), and who is going to hear all about how my son and daughter are involved in this opportunity and how this product may help his family with jet lag and keeping their immune systems strong while they travel. In a few minutes they will be bringing our snacks and it will be a wonderful window of opportunity for me to connect a little more.

When I first became involved with Cell Tech, Daryl Kollman talked a lot about a *window of opportunity* that the Dalai Lama talked about, and about how we had a small window now to make choices that could literally save the world.

> **If we continue to live without regard or respect for our environment we are going to collectively contribute to the depletion and extinction of many necessary natural resources.**

We cannot, for example, continue to use so many chemicals because we are totally polluting our topsoil, and we are eating foods that are totally lacking in the minerals we need. We will not find peace by making war, but by being peaceful. Unless we start to take some immediate action about these things, we are going to find that we will eventually have to take massive action to compensate for what we didn't do today. That is why I say that what we don't do speaks as loudly about us as what actions we actually take.

> **The quality of our lives is decided by the quality of our choices, and this is evident in our personal as well as our professional life.**

When I was living in France, and decided that I wanted to return to the U.S., I had a lot of options as to where to go to live. I had heard for so long that it was really much harder to be a successful photographer now because there were so many of them, but my point of view differed, and I heard the same thoughts about being successful in network marketing. Everybody is already involved, goes the negative chatter; there are too many companies now competing for our dollar; all my friends have already been approached; this only works for those who get in early. Does all this sound familiar? Well, my thinking is that the more people involved, the easier the opportunity.

When I first started taking photos, the choices of where you could live as a fashion photographer were not so vast as they are today, and Paris, Milan, London and New York were the centers for this kind of activity. Today Vogue, Elle, Marie Claire, and most other successful magazines publish editions in cities all around the world, so even if there are more photographers, there are thousands of more opportunities as well. And now, with all the modern conveniences such as computers, faxes and airlines a photographer can live virtually anywhere.

When I chose to live in Santa Fe, I knew that there would be very little work for me in that market unless my clients came there, because my rates were too high and the talent to accomplish my style of photo didn't live there, such as top models, hairstylists, make-up people, etc. There wasn't much competition in the area of fashion photography but there weren't many clients either. Some very famous photographers have homes there, but don't actually live in them. Should decentralization bring some big fashion companies to set up headquarters in Santa Fe, you will probably see more and more fashion photographers moving there. If you want to be a bull fighter you have to go to where the bulls are.

As far as the opportunity still available in networking, I personally think it is bigger and better than ever before.

Thanks to all the legal battles won by Amway, network marketing has finally not only gained acceptance but is being accepted as a respected way to do business. Most of the people who say they are against it are just not understanding it because they haven't been educated about its real essence. As more and more families want the experience of spending more time at home, as more and more people want to work to create their own wealth rather than somebody else's, more and more people will gravitate towards what we are doing. As every year hundreds and maybe thousands of people attain financial freedom and acquire time freedom, our industry will become more and more believable and thus more and more attractive to others. Those that have been down the road, who have built organizations, who have learned through trial and error, will be sought out by those wanting to enter our world. Our opportunity will continue to expand and more and more people will realize that they have a choice, a choice to live the life of their dreams, a choice to live every moment of their day doing what they love to do and sharing their dreams with countless others, a choice to live each moment with conscious awareness and in harmony with their souls purpose.

We all came here to make a unique contribution, and to evolve into fully realized souls. When people see the leaders of network marketing becoming a shining example of leading a fulfilled life, this will work as a magnet drawing countless others to our ranks. This day will come.

Chapter Thirteen

Personal Responsibility

One of the most current dilemmas in network marketing is which company to work with, and is it possible to work with more than one company. In my case, it took me a number of experiences to find a company that I felt in harmony with on all the different levels. Are there other companies that would have made me happy? I 'm sure there are, but my destiny for now is tied to Cell Tech. However, as we explore this subject, you will see that there are pros and cons to everything.

What would have happened to my life if I had just stayed with my first company? Well, I feel I would have a very substantial check by now, but as I said earlier, I just couldn't get excited enough about selling telephone services to create enough momentum. I was an engine without super octane fuel. I could say the same for the diet cookies or the gold and silver jewelry. Each time it was network marketing and lifestyle that I was passionate about. Now I'm not saying that none of these companies had a vision, but the message I got in each of them is that they were about helping people make money, which is not a bad cause, but I would rather make money doing something that I am passionate about. When I joined Cell Tech, what excited me was not only networking, but the product and the company vision, and what I experienced as the uniqueness of both of them. The totality of the parts synergistically created something that not only attracted me, but others like me, and this is what I love. When I get together with the people in Cell Tech, my heart is connected to theirs, and many of us share similar concerns and dreams. Each company has a different flavor and each experience tastes different.

My first year in Cell Tech was one of constant growth, and it was tremendously exciting to be part of that momentum. I saw a window of opportunity and accepted it fully. Then in July of 96, Cell Tech went through a different process. The main product, the algae, is loaded with chlorophyll, which is known to be a wonderful blood cleanser, and our whole nutritional program, which Cell Tech calls the EAT kit for Eat Algae Today, is known to help cleanse the body and eliminate toxins. Well, in July of 96, the company started to go through a kind of cleanse itself, and a lot of the people who had joined the company hoping to make a quick buck started to struggle more with their growth because the cold market mailings were less effective. Many of us had been so busy recruiting, not necessarily sponsoring, that we didn't give the people who joined, the education they needed to use the products properly, and after six months, if they didn't place an order, they were dropped from the computer. Cell Tech is definitely a company headed for greatness, but in a way that will not compromise their integrity, and as I mentioned earlier, the corporate decisions are not always understood or appreciated by some members of the field. My experience is that they are doing a great job of following their vision and not letting themselves get sidetracked by instant gratification.

For the last nine months now, the company has maintained a steady status quo, and some of those that were seduced by the constant growth have started looking for the same thing in other companies. There has been a fairly present ongoing discussion about the merits of belonging to more than one networking company, and a lot of talk about the ethics of cross-sponsoring, which has to do with sharing a second company with anyone in your first company that is not on your first level. In Cell Tech there is a rule about not presenting a different networking opportunity to anyone that is not on your first level, so it is considered not ethical, for instance, for someone that I have sponsored into Cell Tech to come to me with another networking opportunity. Nor are you supposed to propose something to people in your second level and below, because they were usually brought to Cell Tech by someone other than yourself. In my case, my original sponsor placed me under two of his friends, and now, if they ever got involved with another company it would be considered a breach of ethics if they were to sponsor me in another MLM opportunity.

I wrestled with the idea of not even bringing up this subject because it is so controversial, and because, to be completely open here, I am not really clear myself on how I feel about this. Now that I have decided to bring it up, I will share with you how I perceive this situation, and what I see as the positive and less positive aspects about working with two different companies.

Again, let me return to the idea of marriage and let's look at how this relationship works and how it applies to network marketing. *By now you have certainly grasped the idea that, for me, networking is like life, and the lessons in life are similar to those we learn in networking, and the same goes for the challenges.* The solution or spiritual idea that I would follow in my personal life, if it is valid and complete, will serve to help make decisions in my work life as well.

When couples live together in a married state, I have seen time and time again that when one or the other introduces a third person into the relationship what usually happens is that the vase that contains the love usually ends up with some major cracks in it, and that the love gets lost as it seeps through these cracks. If you fill a tin cup with water and then poke a tiny hole in the bottom of the cup, it won't be long until the water is all gone. The bigger the hole, the quicker the water will leave the cup. I am also ready to admit that sometimes a third party affair works in ways that end up saving the marriage also, so this is not just a one way street. Sometimes, the presence of a third person allows one to see clearly the preciousness of what they have, and they turn back to face their partner and end up with a deep appreciation of what they already have. The grass frequently looks greener on the other side, and many of us know how wonderful the passion is with a new found lover.

My experience also tells me that if you don't work out challenges with one partner, you will undoubtedly face these same challenges with the new partner, and often in a more difficult dynamic.

I also admit that sometimes when we enter into a vibrant, passionate relationship other than our primary one, it brings home how devoid of passion our current life is and how necessary it is to move onward. We then have a choice to either find a way to put more passion into what we have, or change our environment. Sometimes a change in attitude is more valuable than an outside change.

Now in my case, I was working in a different networking company, and when I experienced Cell Tech, it was like waking up into passion again, similar to what I felt when I fell in love with photography. I had a similar experience in my personal life. I had been married for a number of years and really thought I was in love with my wife (Susan). Then I met Nathalie and my life turned inside out. Until I had the experience of her, I thought that what I had was what I wanted. Somehow, the idea of having children with Nathalie seemed more real than with my current wife. After debating, painfully, I might add, for months over what to do, I decided to move from France to New York with my then current wife, completely leave my relationship with Nathalie, and make my marriage work. Curiously enough, my wife went to New

York without me in order to find an apartment and prepare our new life. I was going to give up photography and concentrate on rewriting a screenplay in which she would be the star. I don't want to give you the wrong idea here. I really did love my wife (Susan), we had a strong spiritual basis together, and I felt it could work. However, in the two weeks that she was in New York, she met someone that she had known from before and they reconnected in a powerful enough way that she told me she didn't want to continue with me. She had been so deeply hurt by my connection with Nathalie, that her faith in our marriage was seeping through the cracks in the vase. Eventually, we ended up getting a divorce and I spent 20 plus years with Nathalie and we brought four delightful beings into creation.

I am still working on figuring out the connection between the separation and current divorce with the fact that the relationship was built in a way that came from my not living in constant truth and integrity.

I bet you're wondering what all this has to do with networking? Well, let's look at this pattern of mine and see how it looks in my work life. Here I am, working with lots of enthusiasm in a networking company and building a pretty strong downline. Along comes Cell Tech, and I see the possibility of having a bigger family, and I fall madly in love with my new relationship. The grass appears greener, so I jump, and like with Nathalie I am deeply rewarded, because all of a sudden everything starts to work. My heart feels like its home, and I feel that God is rewarding me for seeking all those years. Everything seems to fall in place and even though I am working hard, it is fun and feels effortless. When I fell in love with photography there was nothing I wanted to do more than photography. I lived, ate and breathed the fashion photo industry. An idea of a holiday and just hanging out on a beach was not nearly as enticing as being involved in creating images.

A friend told me that when I left Susan and split up I had fallen on all four feet, but it sure didn't feel like that. I fell gracefully when Nathalie left. Nathalie often told me that I was and am very adept at forming great arguments to justify my behavior, so I want to be careful at all times to not make incorrect statements that justify any behavior of mine lacking integrity. The reason I bring all this up is that I want to fully accept personal responsibility, especially in the areas where I attract situations that are not easy, so I don't want to blame, or sound like I am blaming, Nathalie or anyone else for the situations in my life that challenge me. I did that for long enough, and now have realized I grow more in learning how to thank them for the opportunity and thus open myself to loving them unconditionally.

The pattern I have mentioned previously is the way I would handle the issue of change. *Sometimes change is created by necessity.* Maybe someone abandons you or something happens to you that forces a change. Other times change comes because you want it, and the pain of your present situation pushes you to leave it behind. And then sometimes the pleasure of something draws you to it so strongly that you are inspired to go for it. One thing that I had never really experienced in my patterns of change was leaving one thing and not having something to immediately hang onto. When there was nothing tangible to grasp, like a new job, I would try drugs, or sex or some other form of outside pleasure that would sustain me in these moments. I would not leave one thing for another without a bridge of some sort. From Susan to Nathalie, or one network company to another, there was more often than not something to hold onto. When Nathalie left, the only thing I could find was the children.

My faith was so shaken that I couldn't find the support in God that I wanted, so I felt like I was in this long free fall and there was a lot of fear along with the pain in my heart. As I experienced this apparent downward trajectory into the darkest recesses of my being, I felt like I was really burning in the fire.

I have mentioned before that as I traveled this path I had many brothers and sisters help me and offer guidance along the way. One of my brothers, Derk Loeks, shared with me that I could look at this darkness like the dark depths of hell or the beautiful void that contained the source of all-knowing. As I shifted my attitude, I started to experience the knowing of this void, and I started to feel the fire cleansing and burning away my impurities. I began to feel the wisdom of the greater mind, the one that is the source of all mind, and the one that knows better than I do how to feel the bliss of freedom.

As I detached from controlling the outcome and surrendered to the concept of unlimited potential, my heart expanded, and the more that my mind got out of the way, the more I connected to the larger learning that comes through the heart.

I gave up trying to find a bridge and opened to the beauty of the emptiness. Hanging in empty space, without fear, trusting the unseen with a knowing that was felt but could not be, at that time, expressed, I started to float in the unseen arms of the true Beloved that creates in an unending stream of self expression. I gave up trying to know where I was going and started to just *be*, and to feel what it was like to experience life with nothing under me, no bridge of any kind other than the loving, supporting embrace of pure, unformed energy.

So when I jumped from one company to the next, I was back in the pattern of the safety net, but when I leapt I didn't think so much about where the leap would land. Also immediately I engaged so fully and so energetically, and didn't stop to feel the fear that had usually accompanied such a switch. I immediately committed to investing everything I had, and even what I didn't have, into my new venture. Like in *Field of Dreams*, when the idea of *build it and they will come* came into the consciousness of the lead character played by Kevin Costner, and he built a baseball field in the middle of his corn field in Iowa, I started to create an organization that later I came to realize would support me in living my passion.

When I committed fully to the jump, I burned the bridge back to the other company by giving my downline away to someone who wanted it and would manage it better than I would. I plunged with my full heart into the new venture and all the unseen forces of the universe conspired to match my commitment and help me along the way. I believe to this day that had a part of me stayed attached to the old, I would not have unfolded so completely to the new.

Could I have handled holding both? I'm sure I could, but without doing full justice to either one. I had experienced months of agonizing torment while trying to balance my feelings for Susan with those I had for Nathalie. Neither was nurtured in the end, and I was a mess. Had I never turned from facing Susan–if when I felt an attraction for Nathalie, and then turned this energy to Susan, I probably would have discovered the same potential with her. Isn't every woman, all woman? Isn't the whole in every piece? If I had invested more in my relationship with Susan, what would have happened?

As Cell Tech hit a plateau and took time out to assimilate who they had become, many people jumped ship looking for another express train going somewhere. It was more important to feel the speed than the joy of the journey. The *need to diversify* and the *don't put all your eggs in one basket* mentality was everywhere, but the core believers stayed. They grouped together and asked the company to develop and offer them the things they wanted. Rather than switch allegiances, in return for changes from the company they pledged their hearts. The company had a choice now, which was to stay locked with where they were and how they behaved, or accept and grow with the distributors who asked for transformation. Daryl and Marta more than rose to the occasion, and a steady flow of change began to happen.

Not fast enough for many, but full of promise for those who were truly connected. The changes are now creating a renewed burst of faith with all the leaders of the companies. Not many people enjoy breaking up a long term relationship, feeling that it makes more sense to build on what they have already invested in.

I have had and continue to have many differences of opinions with the Possicks since I started working with them, and one of the most challenging has been around the subject of momentum. I respect the business acumen of Charles but personally don't like all his ideas, and working with him has always felt more like working for him, which translates *do it his way or get out of his way*, and this does not feel good to me. Charles believes, and maybe rightfully so, but maybe not, that once you stop momentum it is hard to build it back up. I feel, why try to go a hundred miles around a curve if you can't control the speed. I prefer to slow down, manage the curve without stress, and resume the journey, stopping along the way if it feels good. I know in my heart that the winds of the one true Creator will always be there, and like a smart sailor you have to know how to place your sail. Cell Tech felt to many of us like an express train out of control, and not everyone enjoyed the stress of such fast growth. Most of the people who were with Cell Tech were in love with a natural substance and drawn to a natural way of living.

Every year almost all of the algae in the Klamath Basin dies, but every year it comes back, usually stronger and more powerful than the year before, because only the hardiest stock make it through the cold Oregon winters. I believe we can allow our growth in the same manner, trusting that the ebb and flow of the universe models a truth that is good for everyone and everything. Many of us had to learn what the Possicks already knew, which was how to manage an office and prepare for the kind of success we had. They were masters at teaching how to grow, but shared little about how to contain the growth. Many of us were left to figure out things with little guidance, which is OK because we all become masters, it just takes longer.

For me, having a spiritual guide allows me to understand things that I can figure out more effectively and more graciously, because he shares with me his knowledge in such a loving and patient way. It was just too painful for the Kollman's and many others to experience so many people having the algae in their homes and not knowing how to use it because people were not taking the time to educate them. I am as responsible as anyone for this but I have since learned through trial and error now what needs to be done to contain a large network. The entire company has learned along with me, and we are once again poised for more growth and those sailing in different waters will not have their sail up in the same place.

Everytime I travel I always try to upgrade to first class, because I am more comfortable there. Many times, I don't get the requested upgrade and so I sit in coach, like right now. As I write this I can't even see the screen I'm writing on because the seat in front of me is pushed all the way back and I can't fully open my laptop. My arms are cramped and it is hard to type, so the ideas don't flow quite so freely because I am too aware of the discomfort. The opportunity for me is that I have to dig deeper and pay more attention.

Another opportunity is the lady on my left, upon seeing my special meal, started talking about low fat diet and is going home with a tape. Once I was unable to get my requested upgrade I let go, and decided to enjoy this seat. Other than a cramp in my neck and some small frustrations I am doing OK, and I am learning I have some more work to do in this area. I hope the energy stream of this seat is flowing with ideas that might have been harder to find in the comfort of first class. This is no different than thinking about the energy of another MLM company.

> **It doesn't feel productive to always worry about what you don't have, but learn, instead, the art of appreciating what you do have.**

This feeling of gratitude will connect you more closely to the source of all energy, and then it won't matter where you are because you will be in the heart of the stream and the center of the wind.

In the coming years, what I see happening is that the more successful networking companies will branch out to incorporate all the new ideas that are being constantly birthed. Companies locked into one marketing plan will develop new divisions and new products sold under the umbrella of a new plan that includes new technologies. Instead of people wanting to work with different companies they will find that they are can be totally fed under one roof.

After all, don't all the religions have us worshipping the same God? People for ages have roamed around exploring different ways to pray, so it doesn't seem strange to me that people want to explore different ways to network. During a time when wars had taken many of the men in the Arab world, it was common for men to have more then one wife. This way the women were cared for. In today's world, this is less common. Times change and we learn to change with them.

When I first moved to New Mexico, I had to adjust to the high altitude and dry climate, but I eventually adapted, just as the world is adapting to and accepting our industry. In the coming years people will more than accept us, they will be rushing to embrace us, wondering why they listened to so many people who shared their fear and passed it off as truth. As more and more of us find time freedom and create residual income, the mass consciousness will feel safe. Just like there is now a television and there will soon be a computer in every house, there will be someone working from their home.

> **People will let go of the old to embrace the new as they have done since the dawn of time.**

People will realize they can experience right livelihood, and just as when Roger Bannister broke the four minute mile and others believed they could do the same, millions of people will come out of the modern work place which still uses slave labor to make others rich, and they will instead turn to a true vocation that is in alignment with a higher consciousness.

I suggest that you get ready. Learn everything you can about how to build and contain a large organization, put it to use, and when you find a company you like, keep your sail up so you are not out playing in some other place when the winds come again, as they always seem to do.

Chapter Fourteen

Meeting Challenges

Sometime during the seventies I went to live in India. My brother Wick had died, and it really shook me up. As I mentioned before, when I went home and saw my Mom and Dad, and felt their loss and their pain, I felt so hopeless because I didn't know how to comfort them. It had happened not long after my marriage with Susan, and he had been my best man. I had asked him to come to Paris and manage my studio, because he had been studying accounting and my business was in a mess because I had no idea how to do my books. I don't think the idea had particularly pleased my parents, because at that time I was living a pretty wild life. I had thought I could teach him about life, but he ended up teaching me.

I decided that all that I thought one was supposed to do, like grow up, get married, have a six figure income, nice cars, etc., wasn't a really effective answer for me, because I had already attained that and had no idea what to do next. And it did nothing to help alleviate the sense of loss, neither for me or for my family. So off to India I went with Susan, to study eastern mysticism, sitar and yoga. I rented my place in Paris for $500 more than it cost me, and figured that I could live pretty well on that in India. I had a few thousand dollars cash in a bank if things got too out of hand.

As I told you in the first chapter, I was truly astonished to find myself staring at a fashion photograph I had taken a few years back for French Elle, a double page of Susan in front of a stain glass window. This taught me more about right livelihood than any book or discourse I ever came across on the subject. I had really struggled to take that photo, fought over the layout, all kinds of challenges, and here it was being used as toilet paper. I learned from this to start enjoying what I was doing more and worrying less about outcomes. It has been a lesson I still carry with me.

> **I love the way life lessons come to us in such unusual ways.**

This idea of right livelihood stayed in my consciousness for more than 25 years, and when I encountered the Cell Tech vision, the idea that my life could make a difference, that I personally could make a large contribution to this world, stirred these memories and woke me up. I remembered that why I had gone to India was to learn how to help others deal with challenges, and that got woke up as well. And here I am today, living my dream. Enjoying a solid income, every weekend I get to go and talk to people about my love and passion of the spiritual path and share with hundreds of people the value of these ideals. I know with every cell of my body that what I am doing makes a difference, and I feel more and more complete.

My children have seen and experienced me leading a fruitful happy life. They don't *think* it's possible to live a life full of God in the material world, they *know* it's possible because they have the experience. They don't *think* it's possible to make a living doing what you love, they *know* it's possible.

> **If you ever want to learn how to earn a six figure income, I would suggest surrounding yourself with people who do that. Too many people resent success rather than try to learn to imitate it.**

God is waiting for us to open up and lead a fulfilled life just like the universe awaits with joyful anticipation the opening of the rose and the experience of its full fragrance. Most people, given the choice, would always choose the fullest, most fragrant rose, and my heart says God wants us to know joy and express our full fragrance, because when we experience joy, God experiences joy, because we come from God's essence.

I had a friend, in fact he was in India with me, who told me he thought that life's experiences were really to teach us and prepare us for dying. When we died, the real life began. Those that had developed strong spirits and could accept leaving the body with no fear, went on a marvelous voyage of light, while those who had done nothing to develop themselves had a difficult and challenging struggle to find freedom. Viewing the body as a prison and the cause of great limitation, Oliver decided to leave the earth early. I hope he is joyfully experiencing the light he sought.

One does not become a champion only in the moment of victory. Evander Holyfield spent a lifetime learning how to absorb hard knocks and punches so that he could withstand the shock of being hit by Mike Tyson, and once Tyson had worn himself out hitting Holyfield, Holyfield knocked him out. One punch from Mike Tyson and I would be out cold. Holyfield didn't become world champion only in that moment, but in the accumulated and collected moments he spent throughout a lifetime of being challenged.

I didn't build a downline in a year, really. I started building when I was born, working, learning, studying, assimilating and I brought some good tools to the table.

When you spend a lot of time working on your inside, connecting to the source of all, sooner or later you will learn to manifest creation yourself, consciously or unconsciously.

Often many people will all do the same action, yet only one of them will find success. Why is that? What is the difference between two sisters, maybe twin sisters, born at the same time to the same parents, going to the same schools, living in the same house, hearing the same music, reading the same books, yet one of them might become an alcoholic and the other a world acknowledged author? For years they did the same actions, had the same teachers, yet one must have done these actions differently, imbued them with a different inner dialogue, infused them with a higher quality passion.

I don't see enough passion in people's actions today. I don't have to wonder why they have partial success when I see how little passion they put into their actions.

> **An action taken in joy will create positive results.**

People are drawn to people who live life joyfully. Passion is charismatic and like the algae is a magnet that attracts people to it. I love to meet passionate people, and that is why I was always drawn to personalities and successful people. I realize now that I vibrate with their passion. Most people that live their passion do so because they could not live any other way and they absolutely refuse to compromise, because they would suffocate. Passion is their real air, it is the stuff that supports their life's breath.

Champions are not born, they are made. The world's best athlete is Dan Obrien, gold medal winner of the 1996 Olympics in the decathlon. Dan comes from a small rural town in Southern Oregon called Klamath Falls (home of Cell Tech), and I drove by one day and photographed his high school. Isn't it wonderful that a young man from a modest background and tiny high school in a town of 17,000 people can beat athletes that are trained in million dollar gyms by highly paid trainers, given the most expensive equipment? I think it must be all the algae he eats.

Dan Obrien has passion, and that is why he is a winner. He has a deep and rich inner being and a heart that nourishes him. His will is as strong as his passion. Did Dan have failures or was he always a champion? I remember during the last tryouts for the Olympics, not only did he fail, he failed in front of millions of people. He could have chosen this moment of embarrassment to disappear, but he used it instead to mold his character. Champions do that kind of thing. This is how they are made.

It's 10:20 pm on a Sunday night, and I think it's time for the hot tub. I just came back from what was a short trip, mileage wise, but took three different planes to accomplish. I got to write a bit, prospect a bit, relax a bit, think a bit. Another great day.

I have a friend from Cell Tech visiting me here, Jacqueline Van Loon. She came to Santa Fe to visit her two sons and is using the house. Our kids get along really well, and we get along really well. I was watching her in the hot tub, relaxing with her eyes closed, and I realized how much power there is in softness. The soft waters of the Colorado River wore out the rocks of the Grand Canyon. I was happy to reconnect with her, because I like the experience of how she combines passion and power in such a soft and loving way. At dinner we had played a little game of role playing around a telephone call and the subject was overcoming objections, and I experienced her agreeing with every objection I had. Always soft, always smiling, always very loving and tender, I got to experience how powerful it is to gently guide people to where you want to take them rather than using brute force.

> **Passion and love creates power; fear creates force.**

Not to long ago I used to respond to people by taking an opposing point of view. I told you that Nathalie would mention how adept I was at winning arguments, so if someone would say it's black, even if I agreed with them I would say it's not black, and set out to prove it. Jacqueline and I were talking with Joan, who lives in my house and helps take care of the younger kids, and Joan was remarking about a friend of mine who has this same quality. We both were masters at taking any side of any argument, and justifying, for us at least, our point of view. The exercise has some value because it causes us to explore all sides of the hologram, and things do look different from different angles. However, this is in opposition to what Jacqueline does. I noticed that what she does embraces the person she is talking with and creates unity (*Yes, I feel just like that*), while what I was doing (*No, you're wrong, that's not how it is*) creates separation. In fact, it drove Nathalie away, so I won the battle and lost the war. One way opens the path for the expression of love, the other closes it. There is no such thing in the world as someone that doesn't have love in their heart, there are only those whose love is blocked.

You can never not be an expression of Divine Love. You can deny it, forget it, not accept it, but as far as I'm concerned we are all created from the same limitless substance of pure and unconditional love.

In order for passion to be effective, there should be some sort of focus. All energy becomes more manifested when it is more clearly focused. Most great accomplishments are attained with a clear and focused passion directed with a strong faith in a particular direction.

Ghandi is an example of clear and focused passion, and with it he changed the direction of a nation. He was willing to die for what he believed in, and he was also willing to live for it, truly live, with a total belief and commitment.

Many people yearn for a cause to live for. We are all divine beings, and our soul's quest is for growth. Nature grows without effort, with a natural tendency to become more. The most beautiful things in nature are those that grow effortlessly. They radiate beauty and balance and harmony. We have made life a struggle, and this struggle deforms us. Put a cover on grass, deprive it of sunlight, and it will suffocate and die. When we wrap ourselves in fear, we stifle our spirit, when its natural tendency is to reach always for expansion.

When we take action born from a should rather than created out of a free flowing expression of pleasure, we don't model anything of great value nor accomplish much. Our spirit, our soul, our very essence is being deprived of its natural tendency of full expression. When this happens, our love is blocked, and in some part of ourselves we feel the pain, consciously or unconsciously. People walk around depressed because they feel disconnected from the pure energy that comes from love, love of who they are and where they come from. What kind of gift is this to offer to God after all he has given us?

Last night in my hotel I watched a fourteen year old skater called Tara become the youngest world champion in skating history. What struck me was that the older the girls got, the less joy they seemed to express in their movements. This young girl was just a bundle of smiles. She seemed to really be having fun. I wondered how many hours of focused energy she had put into her young life, and how she could learn so much in so few years. Young champions are springing up in all the sports now, boys and girls dominating what used to be an adult world. From tennis to the gym, from the pools to some other arena, teenagers are showing us the possibility of expanded potential. As more young people make breakthroughs, others know the possibility. Maybe one day we'll have a teenage, culturally diverse, female president because the kids today believe anything is possible.

When Charles introduced me to Cell Tech and showed me how to play big, I could see the possibility because he had already done it. Most people don't have big networks because they don't really believe that it is possible for them. And guess what? *If you don't believe it is possible, it isn't.* By actually witnessing and experiencing Charles and Kare's network, by having them do three ways with new people, I exposed this possibility to most of my first level builders who caught the vision and became double diamonds. People didn't know that you could mail tapes and sign up strangers. They thought that network marketing meant opportunity meetings that you invited people to without telling them too specifically what they were coming to, and that you had to hound your friends into submission. So when people were exposed to a new paradigm, and they could actually talk to people who were doing it, the belief level of people believing they could do it increased dramatically.

It is often said that there are many ordinary people making extraordinary incomes in network marketing, because anyone can do it. We all do it anyway, because it is a natural tendency to share, but we don't always get paid for it. When I stop someone on the street to ask them for a good local restaurant, they don't get a commission for sending me to a certain place. They don't even get a thank you, from the restaurant, that is. (They always get one from me.) People don't like to withhold information, they like to share it. I used to have a really hard time to hold confidences, because I have such a yearning to share information. I still do. I want total knowledge for others as much as I want it for myself. Because I am a part of everyone, I can not be complete until everyone is complete. Some part of me remains undeveloped unless everyone develops.

So during a training, when someone makes a breakthrough, when someone's passion gets awakened, the whole universe subtly can feel this change. If I stub my little toe, I still feel it even though it is an outside extremity of my being, and as Charlotte in Minneapolis gets excited about her business again, somewhere, someone else feels this excitement because Charlotte is a part of the universal body.

As I grow, I accept more and more that everything in my life is self-created. This does not mean that I am always consciously aware of what I am doing, because I do not live every moment with conscious awareness, even though this is my intention. But I am learning more and more about the benefits of consciously focusing on positive things rather than allowing negative thought patterns to dominate my consciousness.

I said before that for years I lay awake at night worrying about what was going to happen to me and the kids and how was I going to support them, and how was I going to help them feel connected and have a sense of family. This was just imagined pain, because none of it came to be. Fortunately, I was guided to a different expression and more productive thinking. No wonder I had heartburn and massive indigestion problems all the time, it was impossible to digest what was happening in both my inner and outer world, so why would my physical world be any different?

> **If we consciously remember that we all come from the pure unconditional love of the Divine, then we will know that it does not serve us to create a feeling of separation from this source by filling our minds with negative thoughts.**

Thought is a pure form of energy, and we can direct this energy by focusing our thoughts. Once you have built an imagined chair, it becomes more and more challenging to change its form. If you change it to what you want before you construct it, it takes very little effort.

When I built my network, when I conceived it in my mind, I didn't know enough about what it would be like to manage it. I did envision having a lot of independent, self-starters who would not need baby-sitting or caretaking, but I still found that there were many aspects I overlooked.

I have built a number of additions on my house, and it is only when they are actually existing in a solid form that I have the experience of certain things and then realize that it would have worked better if this window had actually been a door that opened, and that there should have been another two feet of width to a certain room. Once you have put a roof on a room, it is not too bad to change a window to a door, but adding another two feet of length can create some challenges. It would have taken very little effort to extend the room out on the drawing plans in proportion to the effort needed later.

> **It is useful to have guides and teachers as you go down certain paths.**

A good architect will know from previous experience that the window should be a door and that you will enjoy your space more with the two extra feet.

My beloved Sidi knows what awaits me on the inner journey, so when I sense a warning of something that doesn't feel right, he can guide me to look deeply at something I might not think to look at. He never goes where he is not invited, doesn't offer advice unless asked, and doesn't interfere with your decision, even if he knows it is not going to take you where you think you want to go. Because of his unlimited faith, he can always be totally accepting and totally allowing of everything. He makes suggestions, will give directions if asked, but has left me to my own devices to figure things out for myself. This way I get the full taste of my experience, rather than just an idea of what might have happened.

An example of this would be that during the moments of my great struggle over feeling abandoned, he constantly told me to take care of myself and my children, to focus my energy on myself and the kids, and to leave Nathalie alone. For months, even years, I would call him on a regular basis and end up always talking about Nathalie and what she was doing. With infinite patience, never admonishing me, he would always listen and lovingly, gently encourage me to turn my focus on myself. Thinking back, I can hardly believe I never frustrated him, but if I did, he never showed it. When I felt strong about something, it seemed he always allowed me to go explore it. I know that Sidi sees things that I cannot see yet, and has a way of knowing the way things will turn out, but he still allows me to experience self-discovery.

I have had similar experiences in my network. Ron and Linda Kalvin, when they first started, tried a number of different things that didn't really work effectively. Both Pete and myself would feel terrible when they would try something new without good results, spend quite a bit of money, and get no apparent return. We both were having great success duplicating what Charles and Kare were doing, but these were independent folks, which is why they are double diamond now. Eventually, by consistently exploring and not letting lack of success stop them, they discovered a list that pulled almost double what current lists were providing, so in the end, they got what they wanted.

Now, maybe if Pete and I had tried to control their experience, they would have done it our way rather than theirs and never discovered the gem they did. There is also the even stronger possibility that they wouldn't have listened to us anyway. They don't need to depend on anyone to tell them how to do something.

> **Because of all the different avenues they explored, they have learned for themselves what works and what doesn't and they have self-reliance and independence.**

Vallerie and John Doell are the same way. They live up in Canada and are the couple I mentioned that built through home parties. They always do what they want and what feels right to them. They have networked for years and enjoy the experience of diversity. Vallerie has a separate business of colon cleansing, John builds houses, and they also are involved in other networking opportunities. Personally, I would love it if they focused all their wonderful energy on Cell Tech alone, and I believe it would cause their business to grow expansively, but they prefer to be diversified and not put all their eggs in one basket.

Michael Jordan wanted the experience of playing baseball, and wisely, I believe, the Chicago Bulls supported him in this decision. Even though they could have resisted more, it wouldn't have been very effective and probably left a very bad taste in Michael's mouth. In the end, he came back to the Bulls and is still leading them to world championships, mostly, I imagine, because his baseball experience didn't satisfy as fully as he anticipated, and he still had a good rapport with the Bulls.

I want for Vallerie and John what works for them and what nourishes them the most. It doesn't serve anyone to have them not feeling really good, so I leave them the space to do whatever they want and try my best to support them in a loving way.

When people in my downline tell me that they want to do something else, if they ask me my opinion, I will always give it. In fact, I sometimes give it even if they don't ask, but I 'm working on this.

Fortunately I have the experience of Sidi and can feel how good it is when someone leaves you a lot of space, so it is getting easier to do this.

> **The more space I am able to leave other people, especially my children, the closer I feel to them.**

When I worked as a photographer, I always seemed to create more powerful pictures when people would give me the idea of what they wanted and then allowed me to co-create it with them. I always felt restricted if someone didn't trust me enough to try new things. Sometimes, I would try something and it wouldn't work, but those clients who stayed in a positive frame of mind, and just encouraged me to keep exploring, always got the best out of me. This works better because it is a more loving way to create. Pure, unconditional love is always present, even when we can't feel it. And when we get our egos out of the way, love expresses itself more freely because there is nothing getting in the way. If we want to receive love, we must learn how to express it ourselves. So when I was taking photos, sometimes I would have to try first to do it my clients way, even when I felt there was a better way, because this was the most loving thing I could do at the time. By giving them what they thought they wanted, it opened the pathway of communication. Sometimes, because the time might be short (the sun might be falling), the most loving thing I could do would be to take control and do it my way, not taking much time to explore their idea. I have been taking photos for over twenty five years, many of those years on a daily basis, so I have already tried a lot of things that others have not yet explored. If I know that their way will not produce the results they want, if I don't have the time to show them this, I would not hesitate to contradict them. In the end, they hired me because they needed results. So if someone in my downline says they have three months until their money runs out and they have to get a *real job*, then I might nudge them harder than someone without this limitation.

What I love about our business is that there is no one system that works everywhere, with the possible exception of always doing the most loving thing. Knowing what is the most loving thing is the challenge. Each and every encounter is a new experience, with each person bringing the magic of their own uniqueness. This allows for a constant stream of new expression. We learn to pay attention to the miracle of every moment, to experience the world in a grain of sand, to know the Divine in every expression.

Chapter Fifteen

Self-Esteem

I have never liked the feeling of people placing restrictions upon me or trying to control me. I believe that I have unlimited potential, and with this unlimited potential comes responsibility.

When someone is ready to assume this responsibility, they don't need someone else telling them what they have to do. Even if they are not ready to assume personal responsibility for their lives, unless they are left a lot of freedom, how are they going to develop the skills they need to assume it? Too much comfort tends to turn people into vegetables. Take away the necessity of making decisions from people and you have a sure way to stunt their growth, because learning to make choices is so vital in our lives.

> **One of the reasons people shy away from making decisions is that they are scared that if they decide incorrectly that the outcome could bring suffering.**

We automatically assume that suffering leads to great pain, but suffering can also lead to great joy. I have definitely suffered in my life, but the outcome now sure feels good. The pain I felt was just the shell around my heart breaking, as Khalil Gibran says, and releasing my heart to expand out to more fullness. It is hard to experience joy with a closed heart.

Often, people tend to hang on to their suffering for a long time. I know, because I did it. But being a victim took so much energy, and didn't make me feel good. I have spent too much of my life pleading for love, and it doesn't work. I have learned that I get held more often when I am not needy. In fact, the more I grow, the more it seems there are arms that embrace me. The way to find love is to love. Why allow the past to erode your future? When you do that you can't be totally present with someone, because a part of you is always somewhere else.

> **Everyone has their moments of sorrow, and we have all been humbled by pain. By carrying this with you, what happens is that your point of focus is never concentrated totally in the moment, and this creates feelings of disconnection.**

Caroline Myss asks if we should let what somebody did or said to us for thirty seconds or thirty minutes thirty years ago command the whole of our lives? I think that what happened to me is that I was stuck in that place because I felt if I let it go I would have to accept responsibility for myself and my ego was frightened because then who could I blame for my failures and my lack of perfection? As long as I could attribute it to someone else, I was cool. This terrible thing was done to me in the past so I don't have to have it all together today. I don't have to be a responsible parent today because my parents really screwed up with me, and I can't love you now because I loved someone before and they really deceived me.

In networking this translates to: I really trusted my upline, and now I've lost all this money because they didn't help me build my downline, and they're never available for three ways, and besides, the company is all screwed up; they have no idea of how to run a big business, and they should really have a different product line.

Any of this sound familiar? Is this your voice or someone else's that you hear? I've played this game, believe me, I'm an expert at it. And I am continually amazed at how many people, even strong people with a lot of material success will still blame outside circumstances when things don't go their way. I know someone who absolutely cannot tolerate people who complain, yet this person always seems to have something to complain about. I am chuckling to myself at this moment wondering if that someone will know who I'm talking about when they read this. The reason for the chuckle is that there is really more than one. I mean, don't we all do this a little?

I am quite uncomfortable in these situations, and have yet to learn where is my best place, because I start to experience frustration and a lack of patience. I am grateful for the opportunity to experience something that *pushes my buttons,* but I definitely do not enjoy myself and I feel unable to release my love.

This weekend I met a young lady who had a wonderful potential which seemed to be mostly used to try to create sympathy for herself. Her cry for love was so strong, her need so great, that it totally overshadowed the gifts she had to offer. Everyone who knew her felt this drain, and the more she played victim the more she isolated herself, which was really the opposite of what she seemed to want. It would take ten to fifteen minutes to answer the simplest question because she was so defensive, and so misunderstood, as she claimed. By the end of the day I found myself wanting to avoid her, which didn't make me feel very noble. Sidi encourages me to learn how to use what he calls the *loving sword*, which is to know how to be strong with love.

This remains for me a big challenge. I am still in the process of learning how to say no, because saying yes seems so much more important. I love to be able to embrace every-thing God sends with an open heart and not try to control the outcome in any particular way. It's a well known fact now that children hear thirty-five times more often the word *no* than *yes*, and thirty-five times more criticisms than compli-ments. I feel by saying as many times yes as possible to my kids, that they will feel that they can do a lot of what they want in life. Eventually they will learn to say their own no rather than have someone else directing them. I don't like it when people say no to me, and don't want to do to others what I don't like having done to me.

My friend Sandye Pinze just called me up and was talk-ing about a friend of hers who had just been to a seminar and when I asked how she liked it, she said that a lot of people were unhappy because some people had gotten more person-al attention than others. My reply was that we can choose to look at our smallness or our bigness and we will become whichever one we choose.

Another friend, Jacqueline Von Loon who is staying with her two sons here for a few days, suggested that the question we need to ask ourselves is do we get uplifted by other's progress as much as by our own, and can we share the reve-lation that comes to someone and make it part of our own process.

Coming home on the plane this weekend there were two ladies playing cards and I remember thinking about how much fun they had. It was because they were more into coop-erating than being competitive, and the energy around the game was so much softer than I've noticed when men play cards. I've been a professional magician and still do a lot of card tricks, and men have such different reactions than women about being fooled. Men seem more threatened when faced with not understanding, and their egos appear to be more involved. Women seem to really enjoy the entertainment, and can like something without understanding it.

> **I am someone who finds great value in competition, believing that it brings out the best in us, and the more talented the opponent, the more fun the competition.**

I am not someone who loses easily because I really like winning, but what I really like about competition is that it gives me a chance to look at my darker aspects. I get to see a lot about my personality through the mirrors that come up in my competitive nature. I have never been as joyous for a competitor's success as my own, so this is something for me to work on. I would love to disengage completely from a result and be totally satisfied to know that I did my best, but this has not been my nature.

What I am working at first here is to learn to appreciate my nature before trying to change it, and so I look for all the good things that have come from this nature. By not being happy when I lose, it has pushed me to constantly improve and get better at what I'm doing. This drive has inspired me all my life to be the best that I can be at something, and I figure if someone else can do something there is no reason I can't do it. I have never liked mediocrity, especially in myself.

> **One of the best things we can do for the world is to improve ourselves on a constant basis and be the best that we can be.**

The desire to improve is energy seeking manifestation, energy wanting to increase, energy wanting to develop and be more. So I see and experience value in having a competitive nature. By being the best that I can be, if someone beats me, at least I have offered them an honest victory. I have heard people say they let people win because it seems so important to them, but I wouldn't want a win like this because it honors no one. Some of these people might have issues over being able to accept success.

As I'm writing this I'm watching a tennis match and it is in the third set and has gone to a tie break. The announcer is talking about a player who said he would rather die like a man than live like a chicken. He's referring to being aggressive in the final moments, and hitting out, throwing caution to the winds. Some people thrive at deeply competitive moments, some get rubber legs and choke completely. We all have our own monsters to embrace in these moments.

I remember Ivan Lendl lost so many finals and everybody thought of him as a choker until one year he came from behind to win the French Open and then was almost unbeatable. He became one of the best big point players in the game.

We have many people like that in Cell Tech. For years they persisted, never really making a big breakthrough, unable to create momentum, never getting the success that others seemed to find. But instead of running from their demons, they hung in there, finally learning to embrace them and attain their dream. Once these people gain the confidence and self-esteem that comes with overcoming challenges, they become transformed people.

> **Network marketing offers people the possibility to experience success in their own business, at their own rhythm, working from their home with their friends and family.**

Most other businesses end up meaning you give up these things, spending your time in someone else's environment, working to make them financially free, and at the pace they deem appropriate.

A close personal friend, Adriana Laskin, called me this morning. She has relocated to Canada with her husband and kids. She used to live here in Santa Fe. We were talking about how many people were feeling a bit discouraged with their networking businesses, because their checks had not grown so much in the last few months. This is where expectations can really hurt people; because they all saw me grow so fast, and they started out like a house on fire, when slower times came they had grown use to anticipating growth and bigger checks so they were disappointed when this didn't happen.

I had some great years as a photographer, and some lesser years, but because I loved what I was doing and knew no other way to make anywhere near as good a living, I continued to persist and hung in there. I am using this slow period to write this book and create some sales tools, and take care of my personal life. I've kept myself busy with seminars and doing things that I love doing. Too many people lack passion about things today, and they seem to accept so easily a lifestyle that doesn't nourish them. I know that many people in my organization worked hard and were disappointed in the results, but my belief is that if they stay committed and keep their passion alive, eventually the success will come. And when it does come they will appreciate it even more.

There is nothing more discouraging to me than seeing my friends struggle. I want others to have what I have; my heart is as hungry for their well being as my own. The challenge is that sometimes I end up wanting success for them more than they seem to want it, because I don't always feel they are willing to do what is necessary for it to happen. And if I do too much for them they start to count on me to build the business for them, which creates a dependency which is not too healthy.

How many jobs available will ever give someone the luxury of a six figure income even after ten years on the job, or even twenty. Most people, if I tell them when they start that they will be making a thousand dollars a month would be ecstatic, yet a year later when I talk to them are disappointed. I can appreciate that everyone would love to have a bigger check—I would love to have a bigger check, but I also know that nature has its cycles and when you try to go in opposition to these cycles, it takes a lot more effort that isn't necessarily more productive. We are so used to the idea that work should be hard, but to me, hard signifies some kind of resistance, and I like to explore the areas of least resistance.

> **When all is flowing, everything unfolds in such an effortless manner, and yet many of us find difficulty in accepting things that come too easily.**

I do not feel that the writing of this book takes a lot of effort; just as I enjoy leading a seminar and it flows forth easily. Before, when I was less secure and had more fear, there was a lot of effort involved. As more love flows, there is less and less resistance, so there is more joy and I like creating from joy.

This book feels like an overflow of ideas that I want to share with others, because I think people will recognize themselves in my victories and in my struggle. There is no law where it is written that life has to be a struggle, there is no rule that I know of that says we have to spend our life doing things we don't love in order to make a good living. In fact, most successful people are successful because they are doing something that they really loved doing and they would not accept otherwise.

If we refuse to do less or be less, no one can force this upon us. We can always decrease our needs rather than do something we hate to increase our income. For years I chose to do catalog photography to pay my bills rather than go work for someone else, and even though I wasn't thrilled, I was darn grateful for the income I earned. I preferred taking pictures to doing something else, because I was at least working in my chosen medium, and every day I could learn about new lighting techniques, or different films, or test new lenses, so I was still learning my art. I wouldn't have had it any other way.

Some people have natures that enjoy slow, steady progress, others like mine enjoy speed. I get very impatient when it comes to learning something. I want to know it all immediately. This has its good points and its bad ones.

> **The seeds of our biggest faults can be found in our biggest assets.**

Nathalie was often in a different rhythm than I was. She enjoyed going slowly and being very meticulous; I enjoyed getting something done quickly in the shortest time. There is no right or wrong and I wouldn't say my way or her way was better. They are just different. Some people do well with deadlines, others don't. We naturally found it quite frustrating to live together and have such different rhythms, but my guess is that we were drawn together for this very reason. A little tension can produce great creativity, and also teaches us how to include someone else's reality in our experience, and how to honor both rhythms. This can make for an interesting dance.

The key again is to learn to bless the differences. Blessing something pours good energy into it. When you feel good in your heart about something, this creates a joyful expression and from this joy will come a more prosperous feeling.

When you feel more prosperous, you will be able to experience more prosperity. Always focus on what you want more of, and bless the contrast and thank it for showing you what you don't want. Nature is full of abundance and prosperity, as is divine energy. When you are grateful you are also in alignment with truth, and this will bring about more expression of these things in your life.

> **How much abundance you experience will always be a direct reflection of what you are thinking and feeling about abundance, and will reflect how much you are in alignment with the divine flow.**

If we let our work come from a place of love it will represent a lot more of who we truly are. Most of my life I have been paid well for things I would do for free if I had no need of money. I have taken my best photographs for the least amount of money. It is not because someone pays me more that I am able to take a greater photo. I can't try harder to make it better. I want every picture I take to be great. Pick up a fashion magazine and you will notice that there are literally hundreds of images, but only a few really great ones. Sometimes these are ads for which someone was paid thousands of dollars, sometimes they are editorial photos for which they were paid hundreds. In both cases the photographers were putting forth their maximum effort. Effort does not always furnish wonderful results, otherwise every artist who tried would be great. If success was just due to effort, everyone who tried would be millionaires. Two people can be doing the exact same thing and have a completely different result; so it is not necessarily how we do something but the energy that is inside the doing. What we are thinking and feeling while we are doing something, even though it is a lot less tangible then the act itself, is what produces the difference in results.

> **The divine energy knows the quality of our intention, knows when something is done from a selfless or selfish viewpoint, and experiences the difference between love and fear, because it is the all-knowing energy and nothing escapes it.**

I am experiencing something over and over as I write this book. I just took a break to go get a bowl of soup, and just before leaving an idea came to me that I really liked, and I was happy because I thought that this could be the theme of my next chapter.

The way I write is to express things as they come, and I don't use an outline or have any idea about what I will write about next. Even when I start a thought, I don't consciously seem to be aware of where it is going, and frequently I have wondered what I am writing about seems to have to do with networking, but as it unfolds, it is revealed. I use to take photos like that, not really knowing what was going to happen, but trusting that something good would. But when I got back from the kitchen, I had forgotten what the thought was. I remember thinking at the time that I ought to write down the thought, but the feeling was so strong, I thought to myself that there was no way I could forget it, but I have. What happened is that somehow in the kitchen I started to think about music, and other things, and by the time I got back here, I was in a different place.

Well, maybe it will come back, and even if it doesn't I trust something else will. For the moment, I have no idea or preconception of the conclusion, I or anyone else, will draw from this writing. It feels good to be able to trust the process and to not worry about the outcome.

I remember always reading about or hearing people talk about how a song or a book or a movie just appeared to come through them. I read just the other day that Billy Bob Thorton saw the character of his latest movie, Sling Blade, in the mirror while shaving. I had experienced this energy desiring to be born come through me and be produced as a photograph, and now the same thing is happening, but it is coming out as words. I hope I can stay out of the way because I enjoy this process.

Chapter Sixteen

Living Connected

How do you get from where you are to where you want to be? This is an often asked question, the answer to which is as varied as the ways, but like in most of the areas we have explored a bit, there are spiritual truths that guide the way, and even though the action steps might differ, the inner laws remain constant. What works in one field will work in another; truth is truth and love is love, and it doesn't matter if the outside picture remains the same. So step number one can once again be to give thanks. Giving thanks or showing gratitude is never not appropriate, so if you ever feel lost, start by giving thanks. Be grateful that you recognize you are lost, because many people are but have no idea that this is so.

It is not uncommon to feel fear about going from where you are to where you want to be because in a sense you are going from the known to the unknown. Those that are good at visualization recognize the places they arrive at, but often we have to cross some invisible bridges and it is our faith that supports us because in reality we do not experience sure footing. These spaces can be seen as similar to the gap we were talking about in conversation, where you stay present and focused on a person, trusting that an organic response will develop. In fearful situations, this can work as well. In every present moment we are complete. The past is in the present because it has brought us to the present situation. The future is present because it will be determined by what you do.

> **Sometimes change is brought about by a tremendous shock, and within every shock there is a revelation, if we look deep. The greater the shock, the greater the revelation.**

I think that the greatest shock I ever experienced was the accidental death of my brother Wick. How precious every moment of our life is was brought home in one sudden thundering lightening bolt. My heart and head and spirit were stretched and expanded in ways I had never dreamed possible. I learned how limiting most of my belief system was, and I learned that I no longer could accept things at face value just because whole societies believed them to be true. There was no right or wrong, but if some information does not serve me, what does it matter how many other people believe it? When I went through my divorce, just because almost everyone I met would say this is undoubtedly for the best, I still couldn't accept it because it didn't feel as if it served me for where I was at the time and it certainly didn't seem as if it served me for where I thought I wanted to go. When Wick died I was hard pressed to experience this as a good thing that was serving the higher good. All I could experience at the time was deep inner pain, some of it mine, some of it the other people involved.

Because I am someone who is terribly impatient in most ways, having the patience to wait through these moments of transition is sometimes really difficult. It is hard for me to stay totally present, because I tend to either go back in my thoughts to what I knew or project forward to what I think might happen. I do this when I speak as well. I do it when I read sometimes by jumping to the end. I used to get impatient in tennis matches to get to the victory, in short I was always rushing, as I said earlier. What I learned was that this all has its source in a feeling of lack, in a fear that if I don't eat fast it might disappear. I could argue till I'm blue in the face that I was only rushing because I wanted to get to another experience, but deep inside I know that when you do something to come out of the present it is because there is a lack of belief somewhere that *every moment contains a miracle and every experience contains the world.* If you don't believe this, then you are coming from lack, because you are saying that something is missing in that experience. To totally relax into the gap and trust fully that every moment contains the fullness of the Divine and the Divine lacks nothing will not allow the space for fear to exist.

> **Fear and worry are part of a mind that doesn't feel the totality of its connection with the Divine.**

When I am in the presence of a master I always see how they never leave the moment. Each and every second, they are present and loving, not projecting into the future, not getting hung up in the past.

Sidi says that we need to be the *sons and daughters of our moment*; and when you learn to live like this, totally focused, totally present, totally involved with where you are, never procrastinating what you can do now, then you start to live in constant connection with the creative power. This power is the source of all and the more you are connected to this force the more you can access it, and when you can access it at will then everything becomes possible.

As I write this I am listening to a conference call with the youth of Cell Tech, and they are talking about what inspires them and I'm sitting here thinking how much they inspire me. Their honesty, their vision, their ability to share their fears without giving in to them, their openness to the reality of challenges that are just tools for personal growth is a pathway of hope for people no matter what age someone is. Their ability to share openly without needing to impress is a beacon of a kind of behavior that the world sorely needs. They understand the value of the *why* and know that the *how* is less important. To know by your early twenties the value of purpose and goals is to get a jump start on life that most of the adults I know never had.

Goal setting was not taught to me when I went to school and I attended what were suppose to be the elite schools in the states. I feel that most of what I have learned of great value I learned through my own pursuits in learning; and my four kids have taught me more about life and how to be than the best school teacher I ever had. I do accept that I could be more ready now then before, but what I have learned from my kids has served me in every part of my life. I have seen what happens when you can leave enough space for someone to be really who they want to be, and I have seen how this manifests in a powerful exhibition of creative uniqueness. I am constantly allowing my kids the space to lead the lives that they want to live and not the one I might want. I truly want them to have their dreams, and that is my dream, not that they do something because I think it would be neat. Naturally I get my two cents in but I think I leave them a lot of latitude. I hated being told by an adult that I had to do something because they were older and knew better, and I don't ever want to be responsible for being part of creating this feeling in someone. I have had to make a lot of effort in this area, and it hasn't always been easy.

We have choices to either reproduce similar patterns of behavior with which we were brought up or to decide to do the opposite. I no longer respect the attitude of people who say they can't help it because they were taught to be like this by their parents.

> **We have free will, and that means that we are given every moment the choice to be who we want to be.**

When we sometimes choose the lesser path, we are the ones who suffer the most, because lesser choices separate us from our feeling oneness, and so we have missed an opportunity of full expression of ourselves.

I had to work to change my patterns of behavior that felt like they didn't work for me anymore in propelling me down the path of enlightenment. True, everything we do eventually propels us into perfect creation, but as I said earlier, I am fueled in part by my impatience.

I just had gotten up to go into the kitchen for a snack and Jaqueline and I read over the last few pages of what I had written. We were both laughing because I talk about how the masters always stay completely present, and here I'm writing about listening to a conference call while I write, and earlier I had a tennis match on. I don't consider myself a master so I figure that sometimes my energy will be dispersed. Besides, I like to let things going on in the periphery of my concentration field inspire me and suggest ideas.

I've seen my friend Martine listen to all of nature that surrounds where he is and from this he extracts deep wisdom. Sidi does the same. One day he wanted to go out looking for a walking stick, and had a particular one in mind. Halfway through the second outing, I realized that it wasn't really a stick he was looking for, but a face, and he had a knowing that in going and looking for a stick, he would find this person.

We have to learn when we network to look deeply into every moment if we are to understand how many gifts the

Divine offers us, how many opportunities for personal growth and thus bigger organizations. Expansion is expansion, and when you expand in one area you will expand in others. We need to know how to allow the space to be empty so that pure energy fills it, and if the space is taken by the energy of the ego, we will only attract more ego, and ego is limited whereas the Divine is infinite.

There is a huge difference between someone who says, "I have failed three times," and someone who says "I am a failure." (S.I. Hayakawa).

Look at the sport of baseball as an example. Every time a batter swings and misses, he won't look at this as a failure, but simply as a miss. Even when he strikes out, he is not going to experience himself as a failure; and if he does, he will develop a very negative attitude. One thing is for sure, and that is if he doesn't swing he won't get a lot of hits. When I give out a tape to someone, I don't count the misses, because they are not what I want to focus on. I would gladly give out thousands and thousands of tapes (in fact I have) to have the organization I now have. So all I have to do is repeat the same thing over again, and I will surely have an increase in results. So what if it takes two or three or five times as long. Where else will I find a similar opportunity? It isn't by focusing on failure that we create success. And because something doesn't work, it doesn't mean you are a failure. I don't like everything my kids do, but I still love them.

Somewhere along the line in today's world, people have accepted without enough questioning that their merit is evaluated by the scores they get. It starts in school, doesn't it? Gillian got 100 on her exam final, isn't she a perfect girl? Johnny didn't pass his exam so we are keeping him back a grade because he failed. There is a stigmatism that goes with not getting a passing grade that does massive damage to a child's psyche.

Most parents don't know how to love unconditionally; this is a trait of the Divine, and the child who has not been guided in keeping alive the Divine connection, depends on human love for their nourishment. When this love is tainted with judgment, as is most human love, the child feels more and more isolated from love. I don't imagine the God I love as a God who loves me less if I fail some exam somewhere. Yet what parent doesn't feel full of pride when their child is a constant honor student?

I know many people, and I mean many, who failed lots of exams, just as I know many who had straight A's. I do not accept that those who got A's are living more productive or fulfilled lives today than the others. Too many artists, sports personalities, adventurers, and other creative people never did well in the system, and they were strong enough that the system couldn't snuff out their fire. So many children today have their wills broken by a barrage of constant criticism.

I remember a few years back I asked someone from my past how some of the kids I grew up with were doing, and she didn't have a whole lot of positive things to say about all the kids that were the honor students when I went to school. Competition has its value, but it also leaves a lot of bodies strewn across the playing field. Look at the vocabulary. *We lost, they beat us, you goofed, you failed, we got clobbered, man, they killed us* are just a few of the affirmations we are fed. Sure doesn't nourish me, how about you?

> **Network marketing has helped more previous *failures* find success than any industry I know of. You don't have to be a genius to earn money as a networker.**

Some of the old fashioned qualities work better, such as honesty, a loving heart, simplicity, the ability to listen, the ability to share, patience, integrity to name just a few. People everywhere are realizing they have been duped into thinking that the only way to get success is to go to college for four years, just the way we were taught that eating meat and having dairy was necessary for good health. We all know now that meat and dairy were billion dollar industries and it served the government to allow these industries to get into our schools and show us all these charts, even if it wasn't the truth. It certainly was economically viable and these industries are known to have made large political contributions. I wonder how many billions of dollars are tied up in our education system? I would hate to think that money had anything to do with making hundreds of thousands of young kids hate learning because it is taught in such a competitive manner.

I have read about and visited some schools who no longer give grades. One school in Sudbury, MA had not had a single case of attention deficit disorder in the almost 20 year history of the school. Could the fact that they never force a kid to read have anything to do with this? How many millions are made because parents are told that attention problems are due to a chemical imbalance that can be handled by drugs? Recently my older son Jason told me that at his university the kids who went to these kinds of schools, the ones where there is no such thing as a transcript, are being actively sought because they know about personal responsibility.

Look into your network. *Isn't it the people who take responsibility for their lives who are the successful ones?* These are the people that I think it is wise to emulate. We are an industry where four years of college or initials after your name are not an assurance of success. Here you can find lots of successful people who might have had less school than you have. And you can do the same thing they did. If you don't know anyone like this, look around and go to some of the Upline Magazine seminars. Upline is a wonderful magazine about the industry that produces seminars where top leaders in different companies come and talk to all kinds of people. You can meet beginners and masters and everything in between at these meetings. Call 800-800-6349 to learn more.

I think that one of the best ways to become a master networker is to meet as many other masters as you can. Instead of being jealous of their success, do what Tony Robbins and many others say to do, and that is to emulate them. Watch them, listen to them, and take the best of what they have to offer, assimilate it, and move on to another one. Look for the common threads of success, and there are many. See and experience how they are all consistent and persistent and know how to get others to see and feel the power of their vision.

> **It is not only by watching champion networkers that you can learn, but through observing champions in any field.**

I was taught that the way to hit a home run was to keep your eye on the ball, swing straight and follow through. That can translate to keep your eye on your goal, act with integrity and follow through with your prospects. *Networking is basically simple, which doesn't always translate to easy.*

I heard a joke today, in a film, which goes like this. What can you sit on, sleep on, and brush your teeth with? The answer was a chair, a bed and a toothbrush. The point here is that we don't see the obvious, and our minds tend to complicate things. We take something that is simply sharing something we are passionate about, and because money enters into the equation, we end up with an internal dialogue that tends to sabotage us.

Think about all the times that you have shared something just because you wanted people to know about it, and you weren't getting any money for it. Wasn't it easy to share it? You usually call your best friends to share an experience with them and you don't focus on any particular outcome. I just told you all about Upline, and I have no financial benefits from sharing that with you. The idea is simple to share, and easy.

Imagine though, that I had a commission given to me from everyone that goes to those seminars. I would have to make sure that you gave some reference when you called in and you would know that I was making some money from recommending the seminars to you. This seems to bring up a lot of complications for people, especially where their friends are involved.

Sexual energy will create a similar complication. Men and women who have been friends will find that if one person has romantic feelings that are not reciprocated, it can create challenges in the relationship. When we try to share love in any form with those we love, there are feelings of rejection when the love is not received. These feelings of rejection come from years of patterns we develop by creating expectations.

When we share anything with the expectation of a certain outcome we immediately set ourselves up for challenges. What happens when we hold the idea of an outcome is that we cannot be totally present because a small part of us is already engaged in the future. The problem is that you can't do something in the future. Try to pick this book up in one minute. You can't do it unless you wait for one minute. And just holding the thought is going to interfere with this moment.

Next time you share your opportunity with a friend, detach from the financial aspect. How would you share this opportunity if there were no finances involved? What would it feel like, how would you explain it differently? What would your heart experience, what would your mind be thinking?

I used to have major challenges with charging money for things, and in some cases I still do. Nathalie had challenges also. She was so uncomfortable with taking money from people that she would put in major overtime on every job. When people hired me to take photos, I would constantly give more than was demanded because I was uncomfortable with how much money I was given. But as I became more comfortable the biggest difference was that I stopped trying so hard and actually started to enjoy myself while taking photos, and when I enjoy what I do, I tend to do it better. Now that I already have a big downline, I am less attached to the outcome when I share my opportunity. In fact, more often than not, if I want anything I want it for the other person.

> **The more I detach from the result, the more I seem to have fun with the experience.**

The more I want what is good for the other person, the better the experience is. The best of all, for me, is when I just do the action or share the experience and not get involved with the outcome. This is true whether I am introducing the products or telling a friend about a film I saw or a book I have read. I used to be really upset when I liked something that someone else didn't like and I would take it personally. Because my ego was involved, my self esteem would go down when people didn't like what I did or said or thought.

I think that if people can figure out a comfortable way to share their products with their friends without worrying, they will have a key to opening a part of themselves and not only will their business improve, but their relationships as well. Wouldn't you rather buy some products you use and put some money in your friends pockets rather than in someone's pocket you don't even know? Wouldn't you feel good about supporting some of your friends financially if you could?

You know what your intention is when you introduce your dream to someone else, and if you know in your heart that you believe in what you are doing, you should develop the inner strength to not let other people's negative thoughts bring you down.

> **The more you connect your feelings to your own set of values, and the more you allow your life to be determined by your integrity, the less you can be pulled off course by others.**

It is not the doubting people in your life who are going to take care of you if you don't follow your dreams; it is not the people who don't trust you now that will be there later either. Try talking totally truthfully to your friends when you are bothered by the money issue. Share with them that you want them to get involved but you feel awkward about the issues of money and ask how they feel about it.

When I first started sharing networking with friends, I was always surprised by who said *yes* and who said *no*. The surprises came because I had expectations. Instead of projecting some response, look at your own integrity. How good, how clean and pure do you feel about what you're doing, and how honest are you with yourself? If you love your products, if you love what you are doing, if you love why you are doing it, and if you have an open loving heart you will also have a loving experience.

Chapter Seventeen

Hope

There are few things that fuel the human heart as fully
as hope. My life felt like it began again when hope
came alive. It was like being reborn. The energy that comes
to us through hope nourishes the spirit the way our algae
nourishes the body. When one part of us is nourished or challenged, there is a ripple effect, so when my spirit feels uplifted, my body reaps benefits, and when I am stressed spiritually, my body is taxed. When we laugh, the chemical balance
in our body is altered, and when we are physically challenged our emotional body is taxed. Just as we are all connected to each other, the different aspects of ourselves are
connected, and what affects one part, affects many.

> **Every moment of existence contains the
> total truth.**

God is in everything, the source of everything, the container of everything; and with God everything is possible.
Every moment of our lives has within it the potential to bring
total change and transformation to us or to people we touch.
Within the heart of this Divine potential exists the seed of

unlimited possibility and the total freedom to become who we want to become. This is what hope is about.

The first time I went to India I made a couple of short films, one which was about daily activity as a form of prayer. The film showed how certain gestures, like those used for ablutions, were repeated in certain activities. Certain movements of sacred rituals, like those used in yoga, were remarkably similar to some normal gestures used during the performance of simple daily tasks.

A friend of mind at the time, Louis Malle, was also making a series of documentary films about India. Louis was a very talented French film maker with world wide recognition so he was getting a lot of assistance from the Indian tourist board and the government; and this gave him information that was helpful to him in having deep insights that affected him deeply.

I remember a very deep discussion with him one day about the subject of hope. He had done one short film on the new housing developments in Calcutta for the poor. He told me that one would think that this was a really great thing that was happening, with government subsidized housing for the poor, but unfortunately, the more apartment buildings that were built, the greater the problem became. This was because for every 500 people that got a place to live, 1500 would show up waiting for their place. Hope of a better life was a powerful magnet that was difficult to find in the rural areas around Calcutta, so when people felt the pull they went to where they were pulled.

This was the time of the Bangladesh crisis, and the government of India was apparently spending over one million dollars a day to just give the refugees bread and water. I visited a camp there and saw five to ten families living together huddled under huge drainpipes. This was the first time in my life that I had really experienced anything like this, and it was disturbing.

Our guide went on to tell me that even though this was one of the model camps (the others were off limits to press and public), and even though the average age was only around 30, over 80% of these people would die within two years because of disease and malnutrition. This visit has stayed in my consciousness for years now, and is one of the reasons I am so happy to be involved with Cell Tech's Solution program because it gives me the opportunity to really do something about situations like this.

Just like an excess of one of our qualities can become a darker energy, the same is true of hope. I am surprised to find myself thinking that too much hope could bring challenges, but that is what happened in India and I have since seen other situations quite similar. When someone finds a solution to this kind of challenge, through the power of networking, the whole world will be able share in this knowledge. Many of us involved in the network marketing industry hold the vision that providing a means of income is vital to overcoming poverty. It is more important to give someone self-esteem and the ability to make a living than giving them food and housing. This is not to downplay the great gifts inherent in helping others, but to offer another gift to make the whole experience complete.

I have said repeatedly that what we do is not as important as who we are while we do it. In other words, what is in our hearts and minds as we do something affects deeply the quality of the doing. We always have the choice of choosing our reaction.

This morning a friend called me up who is walking in the fire over issues with a friend with whom she is living who is unable to let go of an old relationship with another woman, and his heart is closed for the moment, and he is unable to share with her a love that she finds nourishing. This is making her angry and frustrated. The man is someone who has a very contradictory nature. I know this because I used to live like this myself. I think I mentioned this not long ago. If she says she thinks something is white, he will take the opposing viewpoint. When she talked about the situation I could feel their pain, and it reminded me of my own when I was living with Nathalie after the breakdown of our marriage. I was so angry and judgmental over everything, and constantly blaming her (just as my friend was blaming this man) that it never felt good for her to be in my presence. So I pushed away what I thought I wanted, just as she is doing. I suggested that she try to use this as an opportunity to love unconditionally, and thus, even if the relationship didn't appear to work, she might become enlightened. So every time he did something to annoy her, she could say to herself, "Great, another chance for me to grow bigger." She laughed at this, but I could feel the renewed presence of hope.

When things aren't going as you would like while you are building your business, always look for what you can do to plug into hope. Remember the first days, when you were so enthusiastic, and this time hold on to the dream. Look what happened to all the people from the sixties who let the dreamstealers rob them of their dreams. How many of them went on to lead fulfilling dreams? And then look at the people who didn't let their dreams die, who hung in there, and finally got what they wanted. Some might not have even reached their dream, but look at how rich their life is.

> **Hope is worth more than anything, and when I look for people to work with me now, I always look to be sure that they still dream.**

Too many people have given up and no longer really believe that success is their birthright. When people are motivated from within, when they experience my opportunity as a path to reach their highest dreams and live the strongest ideals, I don't need to constantly motivate them through challenges by incentive motivation tactics because they want their dream more than they want money. Money is an energy form to assist us in realizing things, and I love it for this reason. But it is what money can do for me and not the paper itself that merits consideration.

I just learned that Marta Kollman, the President of Cell Tech, has been named as one of the ten most influential women in network marketing by The International Network Marketing Directory. When they sent me the information I noticed that they were publishing a lot of articles about networking, so I offered to write an article on networking as a path of spiritual growth. I don't know if they'll actually publish it, but I know for sure that if I didn't write it and send it, they definitely wouldn't publish it. I am constantly looking for opportunities to increase prospecting leads for my people, and when they come I am going to constantly take action in order to maximize my chances. Here's the article I just wrote.

Networking as a Path of Spiritual Growth

We are all here on earth for a reason. We each have a unique gift that makes us special. One of the greatest things that can happen to us in this life is to be able to work doing something we love and that is in harmony with our purpose in life.

When our work hours are spent making a life rather than making a living, when we take action fueled by passion rather than necessity, we live a more fulfilled existence. I believe that it is everyone's dream to live like this.

The biggest fear people have in today's world, spoken or unspoken, is that they are leading a life without meaning. The reason most people are not facing this openly is that it is very traumatic to look at the possibility that we are not living up to our potential, especially so if once we accept this we then have no idea of how to remedy the situation. I believe that most of us that are drawn to the experience of networking are really attracted to the possibility of change, personal growth and transformation that they feel is possible to attain through this medium. This translates into hope. When people first experience the possibilities that could be open to them through our industry, they get very excited.

We all want to make a difference with our lives, we all want to be part of global change and transformation. But we can't help change the world if we don't know how to change ourselves. There has been a challenge in the modern world of being able to find a business that is service oriented and pays well, that doesn't require years of study and various degrees in order to work in these fields. Network marketing has met this challenge head on and come out victorious. There are thousands of people now living their dreams because of being involved with our industry. This means that they are doing something they believe has value and earning a sub-stantial income at the same time, which allows them to grow spiritual, mentally and financially. Let's look at some of the reasons why and how networking is a path of spiritual growth.

First and foremost networking is right livelihood. What does this mean? This means that our industry is founded on principles that are in harmony with spiritual laws.

It is almost impossible to become successful in network-ing without helping others become successful. I say almost because a few people have introduced their opportunity to just one person, and this one person has gone on to do all the work, built the entire organization while the first person reaps major benefits. But most of the people I see that are successful in our business do well because they are good at showing others how to do well. So this is a cooperative way of doing business rather than a competitive one.

Another thing that helps us to grow spiritually is know-ing how to be in relation to others. Relationship issues are a constant opportunity of growth, and as we learn to be more loving and more tolerant of others, our heart expands. When we learn to honor people, they, in turn, honor us.

My friend, Daryl Kollman, says that the greatest human need is the need to feel connected. Networking fulfills this need, connecting people of all races, color and creeds onto a playing field where everyone has equal opportunity. We all start out with no one underneath us in the business, and our success is truly up to us, so we learn a lot about personal responsibility. When we work hard and are successful, we reap the benefits rather than an employer, and this increases our sense of self esteem. I have been working with inner city ex-gang members from South Central Los Angeles, and one of them recently wrote, "I was raised by the streets of Los Angeles where no one wants to hire me. I know of no other place on this earth that has given me the gift of a legal business opportunity." To be able to share the networking opportunity with people like Casper has opened doors to places in my consciousness I never accessed before.

Networking is redistributing the wealth of the world into the hands of caring people. It is a pure form of free enterprise and a way of doing business that honors each participant. It is the perfect place to live the purpose of helping others achieve success in their lives. Nothing creates spiritual growth more than opening the heart so our love can flow freely, and as we help and watch others grow our hearts can not help but open more.

Because networking companies depend on word of mouth for their sales, they by necessity have to have quality products, because people are not going to lie to their friends and get away with it for very long. When we enhance one part of our lives, we enhance other parts as well, and when you use quality it usually enhances some part of your life. A strong spirit is going to help you emotionally and physically, and if your body is properly nourished by the best quality products, then the rest of you will prosper.

Networking offers choices to people, choices to live and work from their home, if they so choose. It offers countless opportunities of choice on a daily basis.

> **The quality of our lives is determined by the quality of our choices, and when we make positive choices we end up with positive lives.**

When we work for ourselves we are living our destiny and not someone else's. Once we accept that we have the power to be whatever we want, to become something more than we are, we are no longer someone else's tool for achieving their dream. Instead we are the tools of achieving our own greatness, which is the way it should be.

I have had the opportunity to work my business with my 20 and 21 year old who in turn have reached the highest level in our company, the youngest ones ever to do so. For those of you who have children you know what this has done for my heart. I have seen many families experience extraordinary healing by being able to work together.

You cannot have an organization bigger than you. You have to grow in order to contain a large downline. You learn how to honor all different kinds of people, how to understand and appreciate the uniqueness in each of them, and how to give them what they want rather than what you think they should have. You learn about patience and developing the skills of a leader and about not asking of others what you are unwilling to do yourself.

Networking is a lot of ordinary people doing extraordinary things. One of these extraordinary things is creating a team of powerful leaders who are spiritually sound people who built their business by helping other people realize their dreams. There are many people in networking today who have realized that they can serve God and live in integrity, combining their highest ideals and purest spirit without compromising their noblest truths and not only create financial freedom for themselves, but others as well, and they can enrich their lives and thousands of others by sharing the process. They can be proud of who they are and what they do, and know that by pursuing their dreams through network marketing they will be fulfilling the reason we are here on earth, which is to experience personal development and spiritual growth.

> **Hope is kept alive by taking action when opportunities present themselves.**

Now that I have sent the article, I will follow up on it but I am detached from what the outcome will be. What I am trying to illustrate here is that hope is kept alive by taking action when opportunities present themselves. The more that I get involved with the process of this book, the more I enjoy myself. So I saw this as a way to start reaching out to more people in the networking industry, figuring that the more people see my name, and the more my work gets known, the more lives I will be able to touch. I have no idea where this path will lead me, but it feels good and I want to follow my feelings.

Chapter Eighteen

Right Action

We all possess an ability that when properly used is a major key to unlocking the mystery of how to succeed in anything we undertake, yet most of us use very little today, for a variety of reasons.

With this ability we can recognize numerous windows of opportunities we might otherwise miss, potentially great prospects which otherwise might slip by unnoticed, or even a future spouse before we even know their name. Developing this ability will also allow us to know just how to do follow-up that most honors a person, understand where our lives are blocked, and know ahead of time whether something will work for the higher good or not. Sounds interesting? Figured out yet what it is? If you haven't, it's because you're not using it, and if you have, it means you are. The answer is intuition.

We are born with our intuition intact, but because we let other people's perceptions cloud our own, little by little we stop trusting our natural instincts. We all know in our hearts what's best for us, but accessing this information without letting the mind get in the way necessitates staying connected to our feelings, and not many of us seem able to do this with any sort of consistency.

Intuition is one of those things that rests in the being side of our nature and not the doing, and because the majority of the world seems more comfortable acknowledging the doing more than the being, too many people overlook the value and the potential of developing and trusting our intuitions. A lot of the world wants things to be tangible in order for them to be able to appreciate them, and people seem to have a love-hate relationship with the inner life. They confuse natural intuition with psychic ability because they get uncomfortable with things they can't understand. This lack of understanding creates all forms of prejudice and because it is based in fear it nourishes nobody.

> **When people don't understand something, it makes them nervous, and when they get nervous they become fearful and then the fear produces dysfunction of all sorts.**

If men and women, or whites and blacks, or Americans and Russians understood each other, we would have more appreciation of each other and less discomfort and separation. Look at how many people have a misunderstanding of the beauty and integrity of our industry simply because they have never been truly educated about what we do. Thank God that enough people had what it took to trust their intuition and stick with it.

One of the biggest challenges for people to overcome in our industry is the *no* they get from their friends, family and relatives who don't understand what is really happening. When people are properly educated and are open enough to really hear the truth about us, they usually experience a change of opinion. But a lot of the new people who get involved with networking are so new to it that they don't know enough themselves to change another's perception. A lot of the time they are involved because something inside themselves, a little voice, an instinct, their intuition, tells them that this is something good. They can't rationalize it, explain it, define it, or even understand it, but they just know it feels right. I wrote the article in the preceding chapter because it felt right to do it. I didn't stop to analyze a lot about it, I just did it because I followed my instincts, and I am trusting them more and more. When I got involved with my current company I did it because it felt right. If I had asked a lot of opinions at the time from other people, I doubt I would have had a lot of people encouraging me. So many times we read or hear about people who accomplished seemingly impossible things because their intuition told them of the possibility. What they do is honor their own internal dialogue when it feels positive to them, and learn how to shut off the voices of negativity, their own as well as others. Many successful people have felt fear and doubt, but they don't allow it to stop them. So how do you stop these voices? I get asked this a lot.

First, question yourself. Basically we all hold within us the answer to every question we could possibly have. If you think of life as a process of uncovering or remembering what we already know rather than going out to find new knowledge, you will be looking in the right direction.

> **At any point of your life, in every moment of our existence, we have the capability to tap into the universal energy flow, to accept our connection with pure, Divine being.**

Because God knows everything, because God is everything, we have to only let go of all that blocks us from experiencing this unconditional love. So all knowledge is available to us at all times. When we learn something through study, it is from mankind, and we are repeating something that someone else is sharing, whereas when we find our knowledge deep in the heart of our infinite knowing, it is from a non-human source. That is why meditation is so important.

Meditation is the book of life, a place where you can go to find universal knowledge, where you can tap into the large ocean of wisdom, and experience unity with everything. When we experience a unified state of being with even one other person, our hearts rest in a blissful state of peace that transcends ordinary daily living. Our mind ceases to question, the chatter dies down, and the heart opens up and expands as it melds with the heart of another. In these moments, there are no questions, and no explanations are needed because we are connected to universal understanding. We know that everything is possible and nothing else matters but this feeling of oneness. The great leaders and mystics are those who experienced this often and knew how to access this state on a regular basis. Ghandi knew that he could not be separated from a single person or from any part of humanity, and he lived his life accordingly. He knew the heart of every untouchable because it was his heart, and he knew there was no personal freedom until every heart felt free, for he was connected to every heart.

I just did a seminar in San Diego and took time to go visit the place where Paramahansa Yogananda spent time and the Self-Realization Fellowship maintains a center. I was looking through the bookstore there, wanting to carry home with me a tangible form of memory, and opened the 1997 calendar book which they called Inner Reflections. In it are wonderful quotes from one of the world's greatest spiritual masters, and I was attracted to one that said, *"Before the searchlight of divine love, everything is revealed."* Basically he said in nine words what it has taken me thousands to express. The great masters have a way of focusing their energy and their ability to express themselves with such clarity comes from the fact that their heart is so connected to the heart of the Divine. Since they know love in such a complete way, they become love, and we are blessed to be able to experience this station through them and have an idea of what it might be for us to have this kind of knowing.

Through meditation we learn how to focus our thoughts, and we have already seen how focused energy has power. Once we are able to experience the difference between thoughts that lack love and are fear based, and those that make us feel we are one with the universal flow of energy, then we are able to consciously choose between these two thought forms. As we rest more often in a positive state of mind, our physical bodies benefit as well. So we are creators and subjects simultaneously. By the direct action of our will and imagination, we can transform who we are into who we want to be. Plants and animals do not have this ability of self-modification. We can influence them, but left to their own devices they will usually revert back to their original tendencies.

As we progress mentally and spiritually, we also need to learn how to transform the physical as a container of higher thought forms. For the last week I have been feeling sickness in my body, and in the past few years, this has been a very rare occurrence. I have been exploring within myself what happened to me mentally, emotionally and spiritually that allowed the space for this to happen. Last weekend was Easter weekend and was the only free weekend on my calendar for the first six months of the year. My feeling is that I needed to go through this experience and wisely chose the moment for it to happen. As my body has battled with this, I have felt the occurrence of a number of negative thought patterns, and I have struggled more than I usually do to stay focused on the positive. My body is sore, I have a strong cough, and feel slightly feverish. I am aware that I am struggling to keep positive thought forms and that it takes a lot more effort to stay away from the negative thoughts that seem more prevalent than usual. I am convinced that all the toxins that are more in evidence at this time in my body are having a very direct influence on my thinking and feeling bodies. Consequently, I am staying off the phone, staying away from challenging situations as much as possible, and really looking inside. I feel less expansive, less generous, less decisive, less loving. I realize this is a huge gift, for it puts me back in touch with a different reality than I am usually experiencing. I haven't worried much for a long time, and I have found myself worrying lately, and so I have a wonderful playing field to see if I can practice what I share and really make it work. I can look at the worry and really experience it as a very negative state of being, so I appreciate it for pointing out areas of concern and constantly bring my mind around to focus on solutions. When I worry I feel cut off from the Divine, I feel weak and separated from the more positive side of my being. I notice that when possibly stressful situations occur I am more sensitive emotionally and less detached. I realize and can appreciate that good health is one of our greatest gifts, and I am going to be careful about taking it for granted.

I realize I have to stop procrastinating about getting out and exercising more, and I need to make the intention to do it and take the action step. I believe that you can improve your abilities by imagining hitting the perfect golf shot or tennis shot, but I don't think that you can imagine increased physical stamina or increased heart rate. You need to actually do some aerobic activity.

> **Good health plays such a vital role in our ability to deal with stress and be good at what we do.**

A lot of networkers spend hours in sedentary activity, especially on the phone, so physical activity brings balance.

I am an independent distributor for a company that promotes vibrant health, so I want to reflect what I promote. I believe that the products do assist the body in obtaining a higher vibratory state of well-being, and this state is conducive to self-improvement, but there are other things that I must do if I am to optimize my potential. As important as exercising and the ability to move the body well are, it is equally as important to know how to still the body and rest. Learning to rest well and maximize our sleep time is vital to our well-being, just as meditation is helpful to learning how to rest during our waking hours.

Good health is a combination of many things, and as there are many books concerning this subject I won't dwell on it here. However, be careful when you start exploring this field because there are a lot of different paths to choose from. Pay attention to how you feel and to what feels natural to you and don't accept everything you read as gospel. Just as I encourage you when reading this material, take what you like and discard the rest. Your final program will probably reflect a bit of one person's ideas and a bit of another. Be sure to nourish all parts of your being, your spiritual body as well as your physical, mental and emotional one. I have chosen to learn as much about each as possible so that I can assume personal responsibility for my wellness. I like to eat superfoods, which are kind of a new science within the field of nutrition. I like alternative medicines rather than chemicals, and I like exploring new ideas in the field of education. I delved into all the religions before choosing to focus on one, I looked at different businesses before choosing networking when I wanted a change.

I am learning more and more to trust where my heart leads me. I want to still the mind so that my heart can lead me. I want to be a person who lives from a feeling place rather than a thinking one. We all are exposed to similar things in our life, and the difference in our lives comes from our responses to these things. Our responses are where we make our choices, consciously or unconsciously. As a few people learn to go with the flow, others are given the chance to experience what it would be like. As a few people develop their physical bodies through proper diet and exercise, others are given the opportunity to see good health manifested into reality and can more easily determine if this is attractive to them or not. As a few hundred thousand people start using superfoods as a part of their nutritional program, others see the value.

> As more and more people use network marketing as a vehicle for financial freedom, others experience the potential. Every single breakthrough is a breakthrough for all of humanity.

Our thoughts are known to have an affect on the chemical balance in our bloodstream. Through meditation and visualization we are able to send different messages to our cells. Just as every moment holds the potential for our lives, every cell holds a similar potential. One unhealthy cell will create another, while every healthy cell will help keep another healthy, so every message we send a cell is important. The more conscious we are, the more we can assume responsibility for ourselves, and once we know how to pay attention, the more we are free to decide if we want to or not. Once we know how to make money, we are free to decide whether this is important to us or not, but if we don't know how, the choice is no longer ours. When we are comfortable driving a big car or small car, we can make a conscious choice of which one to drive, but if we have fear over driving a big car, the choice to drive a small car is not from an empowered place. We can justify it by saying we are using less gas, and thus we are not contributing so much pollution, but we still have been driven to a choice by fear.

That is why I like experimenting with different techniques in a business, so that I can then choose from what I want to do rather than being forced to do something in a particular way because it is all I know how to do. When I first started taking photographs, I only knew how to take photos in natural light, so consequently that was all I did. Later I learned about how to use strobe lights or flash, so I could then choose between these methods. Still later I learned about using light in a studio, and then in a house, so I had four things to choose from. I learned about different films, and different cameras, and as I grew technically more and more proficient I had more choices of how to create images, and I felt less and less limited. Look at all the periods Picasso went through. Eventually, when he stood in front of a canvas, he had the full experience of unlimited potential, because he had so many choices available to him.

> **Our life is like an empty canvas and we are free to create whatever we want on this canvas. The more we develop ourselves, the more choices we have.**

I have started learning guitar on a weekly basis. Both my boys play guitar and my daughter Tara is studying trumpet and piano, and Jessica just married a trumpet player. Six months ago, I knew maybe one or two songs that I could play all the way through, now I know five or six. The more I practice, the more I develop this side of myself, the more options will be open to me. Eventually I hope to be able to play with the whole family, but in order for this vision to manifest, I needed to take action now.

When I look to my future, I realize that over the years I have developed a lot of skills that I could live by. Each one that I have developed is because I was doing something that I really loved doing. For years I was a professional magician, and I have spent many wonderful hours developing my skills and am totally confident that I could earn money performing. I have lived already from photography, I am currently living from network marketing, and am developing my skills as a seminar leader. I am currently learning about the process of writing a book. What I am sharing here is that I have created a lot of options for myself, and all of them are things I love to do. I have done well renovating houses and re-selling them as well, so when one income stream falls off, I feel that I can turn to something else. Too often people limit their options because they don't take action early enough. I know that I always have the option to go to work for someone else, but this limits time freedom, which is worth more than money to me. The ability to spend my time how I want to spend it is what really excites me.

I encourage each of you to look deeply at your hobbies, your passions, the things that you really like to do and sit down and focus on what it would be like if you could do things you love to do every day of your life. I know that many of you reading a book like this may already be living in such a manner, but for those of you who aren't, now is the time to start.

> **Procrastination does more to keep people from their true destiny than almost any force on earth.**

We all have abilities, we all have unique gifts, we all have the capacity to live richer and fuller lives. Too many people do not understand their own power and so fall under the spell of another person's power.

> **When we fully accept that we have the potential to live as fully realized Divine beings, our choices become unlimited.**

With this realization, of course, comes the responsibility that we have to live in accordance with our realization. There are certain choices that are no longer available to us, like doing things that are out of integrity, but there is still no limit to the amount of available choices that exist. The more we grow, the more choices there are because there are more things that we can do, more that we are capable of.

I like to go inside myself and imagine on a constant basis what my life would feel like if I was living out more of my potential. I constantly question how open I am to change, how willing I am to let go of attachments. I look closely at what it would be like to have a stronger physical body and a more aware spiritual sense. There are still times when I am unsure of what to do and I still experience fear over some things. I mentioned earlier I have been feeling sick this week, and I am dealing with what it would be like to travel to Alaska this weekend feeling how I feel today, which isn't completely well. So I am creating a trip where I feel completely recovered, and full of energy. I see and feel myself leading a workshop during which I really feel great. I know that I must trust that this will happen in order for it to happen, so I am looking deeply at how much I trust, and also where I have fear. Because I don't often feel fear, I thank God for this opportunity. I am having an opportunity to look in places that I haven't looked in for awhile, and I can feel where I have made progress and where I need to work. It reminds me of the time not so long ago when I used to be all the time in this place, so I bless my progress. And it reawakens compassion in me for others who are stuck in this place.

Before my life fell apart, when I was always feeling blessed and happy, I almost couldn't experience what others felt when they suffered. I wondered if I was too detached from humanity, and questioned whether I wasn't a totally selfish person, because I had such a hard time understanding why others allowed negative feelings to dominate their lives. When I was so deeply humbled I learned how big a challenge this can be. I learned from the very core of my being what it feels like to live in this station. And I learned about living with pain. I can still feel moments of arrogance because I am blessed with a wonderful life, but I can witness the arrogance now and ask for forgiveness because I don't like the feeling.

My ego still feels pride, another feeling I don't want. So I thank God for giving me the grace to recognize pride and arrogance, and am deciding to choose to feel love instead.

I hope by sharing my thoughts and challenges so openly that you can feel my heart. I don't want to paint a false idea for you, that once you reach a certain stage all is forever completely well. I am sure that in the end it is, but I still walk in my humanity. For too many years we have been taught that you grow up, fall in love, make a six figure income and live happily ever after. We are taught that when you accept God in your life, everything is perfect. What I found is that when you accept God in your life, the real work begins, because now you have the tool to face the darkness. So instead of overnight everything becoming rose colored, all of a sudden we are thrown into the big battle, *the battle with our ego*. When we completely accept God, we can finally completely let go of the ego, but the ego doesn't like this one bit, and it struggles for its very life.

I want my kids to know that love includes pain, that enlightenment includes suffering, but that both pain and suffering can be a part of us and that we can learn to embrace them. I want them to know that challenges keep coming in order that we can ascend to higher states of consciousness, and that we can learn to embrace all of life, not just a few parts of it. In order to eat a cake, we start with a mouthful, and if you want to enjoy the cake, it is wise to enjoy first the mouthful.

Chapter Nineteen

Facing Change

I love people that have a positive attitude. It is one of the most charismatic things to me when I meet people. I just love it when they radiate energy, well-being, happiness, enthusiasm and qualities that reflect they are enjoying themselves. There is nothing more draining for me then being around negative energy and people that continue to exist in a victim mode. I feel really bad when I think about those recent years when I did that to everyone, and know now that I am compensating by serving as an inspiration because I came from such a negative place to one of power. Most of the people who knew me have to figure that if I did it they can too, because I was really feeling sorry for myself. When I encounter this energy now in others I have a lot of compassion for the people, and know that they are going to stay there until they decide to change. I know that I needed to wait until I was ready; I had to completely experience my process, and that it was an integral part of my journey.

What most empowered me to change was the people that left me the space yet encouraged me to change the pain into passion, and to let go of the thought patterns that no longer served me. So when I encounter this energy I try to do the same thing. If after awhile I feel that there is nothing I can do, I tend to withdraw and wait.

This kind of occurrence is a very familiar one to those of us who work in networking, because when you work with a lot of people you are bound to have a certain number of people going through strong emotional crisis. The kind of people drawn to our lifestyles are ones who deeply yearn for personal growth. They want to control their lives, they want to accept personal responsibility, they want to live their lives as free creative spirits. They want to rid themselves of erroneous conscious thinking, and instead direct their lives by applying correct conscious self-direction.

This transition takes time, and we need to honor the people in our lives that come to us for support with this endeavor.

I believe it is by fully honoring what each individual feels they want at any given moment that we can create connections that are from the heart and thus can be enduring.

If you always, without hesitation, choose to allow each person to live their lives as they want to, you will not only create strong business partners, but lifelong friends as well. Never let your own personal agenda get in the way of someone else's life. I will always be there to encourage people to go through their fears, but I don't want to have them doing the business because I want it for them.

This is most difficult for me to do with my two oldest children. I would love it if they both worked more at their business, just as I would love it if everyone in my downline worked as hard as I did to build their businesses. The financial reward would be much greater for everyone, myself included, yet few seem willing to do what is really necessary.

Everyone would like to have more money, but not everyone is willing to do all the actions necessary.

So I have learned to not only accept that they have another time frame and different rhythm, but to bless this and let go of any idea that I might have about what should or could happen.

I do feel that a lot of people allow themselves to give up quicker than I would, but I don't have as much judgment about this as I did before. I do realize that I love to help people but don't want to do more for them than they are willing to do for themselves. I know that I have repeated this many times, but one of the main reasons that people burn out in business is because they try to do too much themselves. We tend to want for others what we have tasted for ourselves, and so we tend to let our energies seep over into other people's lives. This is wonderful when they pick up on that energy and run with it, but when we end up supporting their efforts so much that we replace their contribution with our own, we run into eventual burn out. If you are the main builder for all your builders, you are not duplicating, which is so important. What works well for me is to use my energy to help instill in them a burning desire that matches mine. Then they run on their own fuel rather than yours and you end up co-creating something instead of doing more for people than they do for themselves.

> **Alchemy talks about turning base metal into gold. This is a symbol of transforming our lower, animal energy into a higher pure form of consciousness.**

The gold referred to here is enlightenment. An enlightened being experiences everything on a higher plane. What we see as base metal, they see as gold. That is the meaning of the secret elixir, and what it does. If this elixir is higher consciousness, the possessor of this can then transform base metal into gold, or raise their consciousness. Almost anything that a person of higher consciousness comes into contact with seems to be imbued with a different energy. They never doubt the Divine wisdom, and so they experience everything as God.

Think what a piece of marble becomes in the hands of a great sculptor, how they transform the marble to reveal a work of art. For those fortunate enough to find a master guide and open enough to become like the piece of marble in their hands, they can go through a similar transformation.

I have been blessed by some great guides, especially in the networking arena. Thanks to publications like Upline, great books written by some of the best networkers in the world, hands on seminars by top leaders in different companies, I have been able to experience many different ways to work in this industry. The principles I apply in networking are no different than those I use as a photographer, or even in writing this book. Persistence, consistence, passion for what I do, faith that everything will turn out as it should, are but a few of the things we have discussed. Sometimes we hear the same truth in a different way, or we hear the same thing ten times and we finally get it.

Prayer is like this. Over a lifetime of accumulated prayer, we are transformed. It is true that one completely heartfelt prayer holds as much potential as 1000 repeated prayers that come from a sense of obligation, but then 1000 completely heartfelt prayers would have an even greater potential. When I first started to learn to pray, it was the same as learning anything else. I first had to learn the words, then to memorize them, then to say them on a continual basis. As I relaxed and didn't have to think about what I was saying, I could put more feeling into what I was doing. The more feeling I put in, the better I felt, and the more I received.

When I network, I try now to put a conscious amount of feeling into what I am doing. The more attention I pay, the more aware I am, the more clues I get as to how I can best serve the person I am with. One totally focused call can easily accomplish what ten non-committed calls might do. Quality always works better for me than quantity. One small moment of truth can be fully nourishing and last for a long time.

Chapter Twenty

Themes of Gratitude

I like to think of every day as a new beginning. Every moment has within its potential the possibility of a life changing event. Every morning that we wake up we experience rebirth. The whole field of unlimited possibilities is before us, and we are given again and again the possibility to change our attitude and thus change our lives. We are given the choice to live with love or live in fear.

As my body has started to get better, I can feel new energy and with this energy comes hope. I am grateful for the last few weeks because I see more clearly how easy it is to give in to others' fears. I can feel how disconnected this makes me feel, and how small. As the poisons run through my body, they run through my mind, and as my body recharges itself with more vital energy, so too, my thought processes become more positive.

I'm traveling today, on my way to Anchorage, Alaska to do a seminar. My body feels tired but my spirit is strong and I am glad to have the opportunity to share. Spending the entire day on planes and in airports really allows me to experience the world. I was surprised in the San Francisco airport to not find a single salad or sandwich for vegetarians. With all the people that travel and the great popularity of natural foods today, I would think that someone would start a chain of healthy restaurants in airports and sports arenas. It is almost impossible to eat a healthy meal in any of these places.

I went through Denver and San Francisco today, where both my older kids live. It felt awkward to not take time to go see them, so I think maybe on the way back I might alter the trip.

While I was in Denver I called my friends Martyn and Martina, two of my front level Double Diamonds, who were back home in Santa Fe. I had a good talk with Martina who told me that her family had been sick as well. Our group is going to follow up on a suggestion of Cindy Bertrand and we are going to start some meetings to help people who are having challenges with their children over issues like hyperactivity and attention problems. Martyn is an excellent tour guide, an adventurer who has been on Everest, the North and South Pole, and wants to lead small groups into nature. We are thinking that this could be a wonderful way to help families learn to communicate in a different atmosphere than a school, without any pressure on the children around performance.

I'm looking forward to participating in this because I know how valuable the product is in helping people who are caught in these situations. Nutrition is so important in helping create balance and harmony.

I bought a little book in the San Francisco airport in which there is a quote from Henry Wadsworth Longfellow. He says, *"The talent of success is nothing more than doing what you can do well, and doing well whatever you do."*

The more I grow in awareness the more I appreciate the freshness of each moment and the inherent opportunity to do everything we do well.

Living every moment as if it was our last would certainly help to make us more aware of how we spend our time and
more selective in our choices. Because I tend to rush things,
which helps me get a lot done, I don't know if I do them as
well as I could. I was thinking about all the finishing touches I could put on the last tape I produced, and wonder if it
would make a difference. I can probably produce a whole
new tape for another niche market which is really needed,
rather than spend time adding music or changing some dialogue. I wonder as I write this book if spending more time on
it would be better. I don't even take the time to reread what
I've written, but I go with my feelings and I'd rather write
than read right now. When I do reread a few pages I can't
even remember writing what I've read, I can hardly remember even having those thoughts. Life appears to be truly
miraculous.

When does fear start to go away? The beginning is when
we start understanding. We fear so many things because we
are unsure of what is going to happen. When we feel more
fully our Divine connection, we know in our hearts that
everything will be OK, because everything God creates is
perfect. If we are lacking in some area, we have the gift
somewhere else to deal with this lack, and that is part of our
journey. If we feel something and don't express it, if the
energy is strong it will manifest itself eventually. So much of
violence is anger expressing itself, anger that was never
understood and never expressed, so it lies, repressed and
seething and festering in the dark areas of our consciousness
seeking to be heard and felt.

> **All energy seeks expression of some sort,
> and powerful energy, like love, will seek
> expression relentlessly. Truth is also
> relentless.**

As we grow older, if we pay attention, it should be easier to sense the patterns that tend to repeat themselves in our lives. From these patterns we can gain a sense of what is here to express the things that we fear and that we have come here to understand. As I have shared with you, some of the things I feel I am here to learn are to have patience, to not judge, to love unconditionally, to honor others in relationship, how to trust myself and others, and how to co-create with others. These are just some of the main issues. I also need to learn how to receive. I am someone who has found it easier to give than receive, and when someone gives me something I feel a need to give something back. This tends to sometimes diminish the pleasure of others who want to give to me, so I am working with awareness around this subject. Because I have been blessed with material abundance, I frequently hear others say, what can I give to someone who has everything. Giving isn't only about material gifts, but they are a vehicle, a way of expressing love that we are comfortable with. I know I love to give things to people, and I know how much love I feel when given the opportunity to do so. So when people give me things, for some reason, in a lot of cases, I am unable to express my feelings of gratitude.

On Easter Nathalie came over to help with an Easter egg hunt for the children. Not only did she bring all the necessary ingredients for the baskets, but a beautiful rose bush for the garden. And I felt so constricted in my heart, I couldn't thank her very well. I am still unable to open my heart to her.

As I travel around the country doing seminars, I receive many gifts from people, and this has been a blessing because I don't really know some of the people well at all, and chances are I won't see them again immediately, so I am left to accept their gift and it is teaching me to be able to accept something without feeling I have to give something back. Some of these gifts are books, and more often than not these books hold some valuable piece of information that I have been looking for. As I learn to receive these gifts, I am sure it is opening my heart to be able to receive love again.

As I achieve more understanding in the areas where I have my fears, it feels like a new me is born all the time, that my life is more and more about rebirth and renewal. I am always surprised each spring when all the perennials come up in my garden that I haven't seen for some time.

> **Potential is not visible to every eye, yet it exists. Can you see the oak tree in the acorn when you pick it up? Masters see potential in each of us and are able to guide us in allowing it to unfold.**

My friend Gilles Arbour saw this in Harriett Fels, the lady who resisted his sharing of his opportunity for over a year. Daryl Kollman saw the potential of the algae as a vehicle for bring hope, health and freedom to people and helping to create world peace, and his wife Marta continues to see the potential of the company and help bring it to life. We need to learn to see our potential. It is our responsibility to ourselves and the world to uncover the veils that keep us from knowing our own unique gifts.

Another thing that I am working on is how to share constructive criticism in a soft and loving way. I also want to know how to share my heart in a way that doesn't feel to people that I am preaching to them.

This weekend in Alaska there were many hearts seeking truth, and sometimes when I sit with people they ask questions and an answer comes to me that is sourced from pure intuition. Sometimes I share these answers in a way that feels harsh to the one receiving, and it hurts my heart to share their pain. I have experienced Sidi tell myself and others much stronger things than I currently see, yet he does it with so much love that for the person receiving the information it feels like a soft embrace. I am going to be more loving in my sharing and develop this aspect of my being until it feels better in my heart.

This weekend I understood how important it is to feel that we are doing something with our lives that will exist long after we are gone.

> **We all yearn to make a contribution, to live knowing that we are doing something that will make a difference.**

During the seminar this weekend someone mentioned that they had done an exercise that really moved them, which was to write their own epitaph. It is probably a good idea to get in touch with our own mortality, because we can make an impact if we choose to. We simply need to start with making a commitment to living each moment fully, being totally present with ourselves and with others. I know that I tend to spend too much time doing and not enough just being, and this is one area where I seek more balance in my life. I am going to commit to spend more time just being with my kids, since they are growing so fast and before I know it they will all be living out of the house, and I will have tons of time to do other things. I want them to remember that I chose to be with them instead of always being on the phone, which is what they feel now. I am going to keep on making this commitment until it becomes a reality.

My children have given me so much. The other night I went into their rooms to turn off their lights because they both tend to fall asleep with their lights on. As I looked at their sleeping faces, my heart was overwhelmed with love and affection. I am going to learn to carry this feeling with me in all moments because it really makes me feel alive. As I gaze down at them, my heart opens to the experience of unconditional love, and I have such a deep experience of my life. Watching them sleep there is such an outpouring of love from my heart as I drink from their essence. I experience all the emotion I hold back in so many other moments, and I think about their mom and my mom and dad, and wonder if they ever watched me sleep and felt a similar experience.

As I write this I wonder what the experience of sharing this quality of love with those in my downline who have given so much of themselves to support me and my children, without actually even being aware of it, would feel like.

I know that I don't thank them enough, and realize that if I did that I would have a much deeper connection with each one. There are thousands of people in my organization that make a contribution to my life that I don't even know and that I have never thanked for what they have done.

I am going to remedy this situation. I am sharing with every one these days how important I feel it is to express gratitude, and am feeling in this moment that I am falling short myself in this area. My heart feels good knowing I can now do something. I love having a plan of action. I work a lot with a friend of mine, Marilyn Hagar, who does a lot of design work and I think I'll ask her to design a fun thank you postcard to send to my downline, and possibly I can share this with some other friends in Cell Tech. I like the idea. Gratitude, gratitude, gratitude! Makes me feel great just to think about it.

I was going to stop and visit with Jason in Denver and spend the afternoon with him, but when I checked my flights I realized that I didn't get to Denver till late afternoon, so I'll pass on this trip and stop when I can have a longer time with him. I am still looking for a way to help him build and keep his downline alive. His first priority is school and I want to help him find a way to really maximize the time he spends doing his business so that he can be as productive as possible. This is a challenge for every networker, not just a twenty year old, so if we can find some solutions everyone will benefit. I am hoping that the new tape we are working on with many of the successful young people in Cell Tech talking to their peers will help them all with this niche market. There are so many thousands of bright, young energetic kids coming out of college that have challenges in the job market that introducing them to the possibilities of networking could open many doors for them. Most of these kids still have their ambition intact and have a healthy attitude about success still being possible. Too many people have given up, worn down by daily struggle, and have lost the energy that fuels the courage to face change and transformation.

> **Never, never, never, never give up.**

I've been reading a wonderful book by **Og Mandino** called *Secrets For Success & Happiness*, which is kind of like a diary, and he talks about his life, his books, his travels, his talks, and his thoughts. He mentions a moment when Winston Churchill stood up, looked over an audience for a few minutes and then said, "Never, never, never, never give up," and then sat back down again. Og wrote a book called *The Twelfth Angel* in which the little hero of the book said the same thing. This man, Og Mandino, has inspired so many millions of people with his books and talks and he is such a wonderful crusader for hope. I am putting on my goals list to share an embrace with this man who touches my heart so deeply.

It seems that who I am today has been formed by reading about so many people like Og Mandino. I have absorbed so many thoughts from so many great people that I have been truly blessed. Every person who lives a part of their greatness helps countless others to do the same.

Every one of us who makes a success out of a home-based business is creating hope for countless others to follow. That means that there will be fewer empty houses for kids to come home to after school, that more families will be able to spend more time together, that more people will be able to live their dream, and that more people will take the chance to explore their greatness. For every one of us who can make a living staying at home, countless thousands of others will have more choices to make in their life, and will have an opportunity to improve the quality of their time here on earth.

Every time one person has the courage to follow their dreams, the positive thought of this possibility floats out into the universal consciousness and congeals with other like thoughts. As these congealed thoughts grow and accumulate, it becomes easier for others to access this consciousness and experience something similar.

As more and more people work for themselves and earn a living while helping others, they will grow spiritually, and the whole world will witness that people can actually make a living doing something they love and doing it with integrity.

As more and more people set an example of living in harmony with their purpose, others will know that they can do the same. We don't have to climb over each other, in fact, in our field the only way to succeed is to help others succeed. In our field a large check usually signifies that a lot of people have been influenced because you took the time to introduce your opportunity to someone else.

I find it remarkable that so many people that have affected my life have no idea of the impact they have had with me, both positive and negative. Imagine the millions of people that have had their hearts touched by Og Mandino, and he has only had the opportunity to meet a few of them. How many people have had their lives turned around because of something he wrote down or said that transformed their pain into hope? Think about Ghandi and Mother Theresa and all the others that have so impacted our world and give thanks to have been blessed to know that people this great have walked the earth.

> **Sometimes the greatest gifts come to us in ways that are hard to accept. It is not always the great saints or leaders of the world that teach us our great lessons, sometimes it is a small, often unnoticed moment that changes our destiny forever.**

Sometimes we make choices that only years later we realize have had a huge impact on our lives. When Charles Possick mailed me that first letter he had no idea that eventually my life would be so impacted. He didn't even know of my existence. The choices I am making today might be planting seeds that I will only see evidence of years from now, but if I live each moment with the understanding that it could possibly impact the rest of my life in monumental fashion, I am going to start paying more attention to everything I do and I am going to walk in awareness every second of my life.

I tried to upgrade on this flight from San Francisco to Denver and was unable to do so. I was feeling a bit bummed out, because it is a lot easier to write in first class than economy. When the table is down in economy and the person in front of me leans back, it is really hard to write on the laptop because my arms are so cramped. This time, however, I was given an exit seat and it's almost as much space as first class and much, much easier to write than when I sit in one of the other seats. Now I am thrilled I didn't get first class, because I learned that every flight I book now in economy I am going to request an exit seat and it is going to make traveling and writing a whole lot easier. Had I gotten an upgrade I would not have had this experience to learn from. I don't know why I didn't think of asking for these seats earlier, but I learned a great lesson. It seems that I get blessed in spite of myself.

I am really sorry I didn't take an extra day to go visit some places in Alaska. Last night at dinner everyone was sharing with me how beautiful it is, and this morning as I was waiting for my ride, I was talking to a bellboy who told me he had moved from Hawaii to Alaska, and that his real passion was photography and that he had never seen such beauty. I had a really wonderful contact with the people here and the seminar included some very intense personal contacts so I am making the intention to come again next year and spend a few extra days to visit some of the places they talked about. I plan to bring my cameras.

As I think about this it makes me wonder about how much procrastination appears in my life and how many opportunities pass me by. I gave a tape this morning to the bellboy but have passed thousands of others and not even thought about repeating the gesture. I realized that I even forgot to pack the usual amount of tapes that I take on these trips so I only had 3-4 tapes to give away this time. It is so easy to let these things slip. I haven't been having the great results I would like when I give tapes on these trips, so instead of looking more deeply at why, it seems I have been avoiding it. These are the times when I know that persistence is important. Never, never, never give up. I am going to make up for it next week on my trip to wherever I go by committing now to give out at least ten tapes between the time I leave home and arrive back. I am also going to commit to giving out more tapes during the week.

My business has been stagnating because I have stopped sponsoring as much as I used to, and this has been reflected in my entire organization. The pace of the leader is the pace of the group, so I am ready to rock and roll again. I am going to set a goal of 100 new people in the next year, personally sponsored. I want to finish this manuscript by the end of April, finish the youth tape, and the physically challenged tape, start a book about all the Cell Tech Solution Projects along with the catalog of arts and crafts to support the people involved, and still spend lots of time with my kids. This is my intention and I am going to let the universe work out the details. I thank God for the vision.

George Singleton should be coming to New Mexico soon to help plant the garden he blessed my property with last year. Og Mandino talked non-stop about his garden and it has instilled a deep desire in me to experience this with George. Last time he was here I was too busy to really participate. This time I want to dig in the earth side by side with him. I want to plant some things and see them grow. In my seminars I know I plant a lot of seeds in others, but I don't often see the manifestation of what happens afterwards. Even though I get lots of calls and letters, for which I'm grateful, I like knowing that people have been helped. It fuels the body for the non-stop traveling.

I am sitting on the floor in Denver airport now hoping to recharge one of my batteries. When I checked in this time, still with no upgrade I could hardly keep from smiling when I got an exit seat again. I still can't believe that I didn't think of this earlier. My heart feels so full today and I'm excited about all the things I want to do. I am so happy to be alive. Tomorrow I am going to start to pour some of this love I feel into my downline. I'm actually starting now.

Chapter Twenty-One

General Thoughts

All life is an opportunity for expression, and we have a moment by moment choice of what we want to express.

As I look around me I see millions upon millions of different expressions, each one chosen consciously or unconsciously, worn by all the people that are walking by me. From their clothes to the way they walk, from the way they wear their hair to the look on their face, everyone sends out a message about themselves. How many of us love enough, and how many feel loved enough? There are so few people smiling, and if you think about the miracle we all are it's hard not to smile, but how often do we pause to reflect on that miracle? We are all like an individual sun in a universe of people, and like our sun that shines upon the planets, our radiance has the potential to illuminate everything around us. We also can be like the moon, and reflect back people's radiance to them.

My heart wants to know the difference between the ordinary and the extraordinary. I do believe it is that *extra*, and I don't think that *extra* is necessarily one big difference, but more often a lot of little things. Our attitude is what makes the difference. And we have the choice of how to react to everything. We don't have to accept letting our past rule the present, nor do we have to accept letting fear about the future ruin the present. It is our attitude that will decide if we run our lives or if our lives run us. The choice is ours.

> **There is an old saying that says those who think they can, can and those who think they can't are right, they can't.**

I think back to the day that I stood in front of a workshop and put my goals up on a flip-chart to use as an example, and discovered what a priority writing a book was. I never doubted that I could do it, I just sat down and started writing. I am hoping I can remember what day that was, and what seminar, because I feel that moment was an awakening for me. At the time, it seemed like so many other moments. I would love to remember what the rest of the goals were, but I didn't save the sheet. I think with all I have planned to do this month I will have to make another sheet because I have so many of my goals that will be reached. I am now 100% convinced of the value of learning how to prioritize our goals. There is no way I would have completed this book without that exercise. What amazes me is that I don't remember giving myself a deadline for the attainment of this goal. I think I put a date to start it by, and I wouldn't be surprised if I have *finished* the book before that date. I leave the flip charts I use with the Distributor Empowerment Team I work with, and I am going to go into my memory and find where I was when I did this, and maybe they still have the sheet.

I have been waiting to feel a sincere desire, from my heart, to start building my business again. I think that this book so filled my heart that there was no room for something else, and before that it was preparing my seminars. Now that both things feel that they have a life of there own, I'm feeling that neither needs my undivided attention. I still don't miss taking pictures very much, and I wonder what will happen with my photography career. If I follow my own ideas, I'll wait until there is a yearning.

My instincts tell me that something is going to happen that is going to show me an exciting way to sponsor people again. I can feel it but don't have a clear picture of what it will be. I trust that when I am ready it will reveal itself. From where, through whom, I don't know and I feel it doesn't matter at all. I am already thanking the universe that it is happening. I can feel that I am going to find a rhythm of life that is quieter than what I have now. It doesn't feel that I will do less, but I will do it with less and less struggle. And more and more fun.

As I was reading Og Mandino's book, yet again, I found myself hearing or reading about prostate problems. I actually called a few weeks ago to make an appointment to have a check-up and never connected with the office. They called back and left a message, then I went away, then I got sick. When I read *Conversations with God*, there was a message about God talking to us through the songs we hear, the books we read, the sound of the wind, etc. I am thinking that I better pay attention to these messages and stop procrastinating.

> So many things in our life can be accomplished by taking one small action today, and the intensity of lots of challenges can be significantly reduced by taking these small actions.

If we can detect something early on, we can remedy the situation a lot easier than at a later date. I remember the time I wasn't paying attention and flew to Raleigh, NC instead of Richmond, VA, and had to take another plane to compensate for the oversight. If I had taken the small action step of paying a bit more attention before I got on the plane, it would have been a simple adjustment to correct, but the longer I waited, the bigger the action I had to take to correct the situation. The same holds true for our health. By making some small changes today we can avoid some big problems later.

It seems at every seminar I go to now there is one or two people who say they are worried about some negative press about the products. As I observe these people and listen to their concern, I am realizing that the ones who do this are really making excuses to justify their lack of success. They say they love the products and just want to be sure that what they are sharing with people won't hurt someone. As more and more people in America realize the benefits of natural, wild-crafted foods, more pharmaceutical companies are financing the publication of these articles and doing whatever they can to fuel any insecurity people may have. Recently there was movement in congress for a bill that would create all kinds of pressure for natural medicine practitioners. Preventive medicine will certainly cut into the profits of these companies, and as more and more people realize benefits, these new industries will build enough mass opinion of their own so that people won't be so easily misled by people trying to preserve their wealth. The more word gets out about a natural style of healthy living, these big industries like meat, dairy and drugs will hopefully have to start telling the truth in order to keep healthy themselves.

> **Truth is relentless. Without truth we can not be healthy.**

I can see the lights of Albuquerque out of the window. It feels good to know I'll be home in less than two hours. I want to look at the sleeping faces of my kids and give them kisses on their warm cheeks. Tomorrow I am going to have breakfast with them. I want this love to grow.

I hope by sharing some general thoughts like this you can feel how I think, because how I think is what determines my attitude, and my attitude is responsible for my level of success.

Chapter Twenty-Two

The Final Chapter

Well, here I am already at the final chapter. I decided in the beginning that I would write 22 chapters, and I am amazed at how quickly I got here. However, I have no idea of what this last chapter will be. It is really late at night, I just finished the previous chapter, and decided that I would just open this one, start it, and then wait until whatever ideas come to me to fill out these final pages. In one sense, I feel complete, like I've shared with you all I had to share. When I typed in Chapter Twenty-Two and then looked at the blank page it felt like the empty frame with the dangling threads of the tapestry I mentioned earlier. Here before me, on the empty pages I am free to create whatever I want. Just like tomorrow with my life, so I think I'll wait till tomorrow.

Two days have passed since I've written anything, but I've been doing a lot of thinking and feeling. I have enjoyed this process so much, it's almost like I don't want it to end. I had a meeting yesterday with my accountant about taxes and was told I have a huge tax bill to pay, and I only have about a third of it. I had really thought about slowing down and spending more time at home, but it looks like I am going to have to work a lot more in order to pay this debt. I know there is wisdom inside this challenge for me, and so I am not going to let it bother me. I am digesting this news now and maybe that's why I haven't yet felt how to end this chapter of my life and this chapter of the book, so I guess I'll wait for another day.

I'm sitting in my hotel room overlooking Flathead Lake in Montana where I've come to do a seminar, and as I look out the window it reminds me of the Klamath Basin, which has played such an important part in my growth and transformation. After so many years of living in cities, I feel good to be reconnected with nature. We are given so much by Mother Earth, and so few people, myself included, know how to send blessings back.

A few months ago I mentioned that I put up a 100 foot greenhouse which houses, amongst other things, an algae pond. I had some pretty important machinery come in and level the land, and I am ashamed to say that I never even thought to ask permission from the land. In the beginning, things did not go easily. Tools were breaking, people were twisting ankles and straining themselves, but immediately after my friend Martine, the Shaman I mentioned earlier, did a blessing, everything started to go more smoothly.

We take so many things from the earth to sustain our bodies, to nourish us, to heal us and often just to amuse us. Once we open a doorway to receive, this opening is not just for energy to pass one way. Imagine if you are in an airtight compartment, and you punch a hole so that you can breathe. This opening will also be a way for more air to leave.

> **Once an exchange of energy is created, the energy does not necessarily flow in only one way.**

If I have a cold and drink from a bottle of water, what is in me can then go into the bottle of water. If I open my heart to send you love, there is a doorway for you back into my heart.

Our connections are all like this. When we open our hearts to accept the Divine energy, we then have a doorway straight to the heart of the Divine through which we can send love and gratitude. As I sit here and write these words wanting to connect with many people, I am energetically opening a pathway of communication that will allow for things to flow to me as well as through me. When I do seminars and stand open in front of people, I become open to them. The more each of us opens to each other, the bigger the passageway and the less chance of experiencing the pain of blocked love. It is important that we learn to love one another and that we increase our awareness around what happens when we exchange energy.

> **Every time we prospect we are opening a doorway of possibility of exchanging energy with someone, and often I see people creating these pathways without conscious realization of what is happening.**

When you go into a situation looking for work, and you don't feel good about being in a certain place, you are not honoring yourself or anyone involved. Suppose you accept a job because you need money, but you wish you were doing something else. Everyday when you go into your place of business you are a conduit of all the pathways you have created, and the other people come in contact with your life history, just as you come into contact with theirs. If you are not happy, you will bring with you this unhappiness, and slowly start to permeate the environment. So I might not know you well and get plugged into your unhappiness, start to feel bad and have no conscious idea why.

Now if I am strong, living with a sense of purpose, vibrating at a high level of wellness, I might not get too affected. But if I am in a weaker moment, I might be more susceptible to your moods. A similar idea would be when your immune system is weak you catch a lot of flu and colds, but when it is strong you resist all these illnesses. That is why it is so vital to live your life consciously, so you don't end up as a tool for other people to reach their dreams.

> **Each one of us has total divine potential. Each one of us has the possibility through grace to experience the unity. It is not because someone is richer, or stronger, or faster or more clever that they have a head start over you.**

Good card players become good when they learn how to play weak hands. When everything comes easy, people don't always learn about how to deal with adversity. For all we know the person born with a physical challenge might successfully integrate this challenge and get enlightened, while someone else blessed with apparent physical prowess might develop nothing more than their ego.

There is a wonderful Sufi saying by Abu Sa'id. When he was asked, "What is a Sufi?" He replied, "Whatever you have in your hand, you give away, whatever you have in your head, you put aside, and you do not flee from whatever befalls you." It is also said a Sufi is a person whose every act is aimed at pleasing God, with the result that every act of God pleases them. In this last sentence you can experience the truth of how energy flows back and forth.

We have a choice when we don't seem to be getting what we want in our lives. We can either develop more faith that what we want is on its way, or we can lessen our desire to match our faith. The way of the warrior doesn't always lead to romance and an easy life.

As I said before, when we accept the Divine presence more fully in our life, that is often when we enter into the real dark areas, but without the Divine, it is an even tougher journey. People seem to think that once you have wealth of any sort, life becomes a piece of cake. It doesn't matter if it is financial wealth, or spiritual, or mental, or emotional or physical. Granted all of these things are wonderful, but because we are always in a process of change, growth and transformation, it just gets relative. The more we become, the more we are able to do more, and the more we are challenged. After all it was because of Ghandi's remarkable spiritual power that he was chosen to lead the struggle for independence. His challenges were magnified examples of some of ours. We learn to manage personal responsibility whereas he assumed responsibility for a nation.

I am not suggesting that we compare ourselves to Ghandi, but that we experience a sense of our unlimited potential. We need to rid ourselves of worrying about what other people think. We have to forget about the past and even stop worrying about the future.

> **We have to assume the mantle of our greatness and wear it every moment, every day, living each moment as if it was our last.**

Not every battle is easy. I was talking recently with Christian Drapeau who is head of the research and development at Cell Tech. Christian has a scientific background as well as a strong spiritual sense, and he shared with me that when people romanticize spirituality that they tend to lose the sense of the spiritual warrior who has to do battle with the demons that try to hold us back.

> **Every time we meet conflict or resistance it is an opportunity to experience where we are and who we are, and I don't think I've ever met any kind of a master who was not a warrior as well.**

Ghandi was a total pacifist but a spiritual warrior, and he went to war with an army of pacifists, and won. It is a huge contradiction to think we can make peace through war. The only way to have peace is to be peaceful. And this is true whether we are talking about individuals or nations. I have realized that for me in terms of feeling at peace with Nathalie, I must let go of every tendency to fight. I have decided to give up being right, and try to feel peace whenever I can.

This weekend a young 21 year old African Asian American astounded the world by winning the Masters golf championship with the biggest margin of victory and the lowest score ever. This afternoon I watched this young man, Tiger Woods, as he walked down the fairways, 21 years old, and with the hopes and dreams of millions of people on his shoulders. He seemed to thrive on the pressure, and it was obvious to me that his power came from deep inside of him. Yes he had beautiful strokes, yes he had great technique, but his attitude and belief are what really made him a winner.

> **I believe we can all develop a powerful and positive attitude and belief system.**

We are not forced to but we are given the opportunity to, and all we need to do is make the choice. I truly believe that every single person has the possibility to live their greatness. That doesn't mean that we will all win the Masters, but it does mean that we are all potential winners. If we all developed our powers to the maximum I don't think that that many people would even want to use their powers to win the Masters. We are all so unique, so special, and each of us has a gift to offer. I haven't written much about my past, about what kind of kid I was, or young adult and how mixed up and confused I was. Maybe that will be another story some day, but I am sure that I would have been the last kid in my class to be thought of as someone who would one day write a book about personal growth and transformation. Sex, drugs and Rock and Roll maybe, but not anything along the lines of this book or my seminars.

I think at some point within ourselves we all know that we are capable of more. As I watched Tiger Woods outperform everyone on the course by 12 strokes, he still got upset with himself when he didn't hit the shot exactly like he thought he should have. Even the best want to be better. The will to grow and be more is part of who we are. The people who do become more are the ones who learn to focus their energy, and I feel that the main difference between people and their levels of success is their level of intensity. Tiger Woods spent thousands of hours intensely focused on who he wanted to become, on who he knew himself to be. I am sure that when he put on the famous green jacket of the Master's champion, he had visualized the entire sequence already. He had already seen, felt and experienced what it felt like to walk off the green at the end of the tournament as the winner. The reality that I experienced today was already decided a long time ago. This was a vision that became reality.

I built my first big downline about ten years ago when I went to that first opportunity meeting in Southern California when someone told me that I could get five people who would get five people who would get five people, etc. and I could retire to sip Pina Colada's in Tahiti. It took a number of years for it to happen, but how many years do you think Tiger waited. I remember as a kid, standing in my bedroom and hearing Vin Scully, the announcer of the Dodgers describe a World Series winning grand slam home run by

yours truly, and then I heard him describe in detail my strik-
ing out the side in the last inning to preserve the victory. But
something in me knew this was a fantasy, because I know I
didn't believe as strongly as Tiger that I would be a World
Champion in my sport. I did not have the same intensity of
desire that he had, because if I did I am convinced I would
have accomplished a lot more in the sport.

When I was involved in photography, I saw myself as a
great photographer in the early years, and took a lot of great
photos. As I got older I saw myself as a good photographer,
not great, and I know now that this was because I lost some
of the intense passion I had for taking pictures.

> **I had great ability, but when the passion
> dies there is not the energy to go through
> the challenges.**

I am passionate now about doing seminars and I know in
my heart that nothing can stop me from being truly great at
this. This may not sound humble, but it is my truth.

I have made an internal decision to follow my passion
which right now is to help people help themselves. I am
committed to helping people open to experience the Divine.
I want people to feel what I feel. I am committed to sharing
Network marketing with people so they know that they can
work for themselves, that they can make a life rather than
just a living, that they can live their dreams and help others
to do the same. There is no need to lead a life of quiet des-
peration because there are many many people waiting to
teach them how to network. I am committed to sharing with
people the superfood that I eat, because I believe that everyone in the world will benefit from it.

This evening I was talking with my friend Kathleen
Loeks, and she was saying that she would continue to do
almost everything she's doing in her life even if she had millions of dollars, and that is what I feel. I want to do these

things because I have an intense, burning desire to make a difference in my life, and because I really love doing these things.

> **Nothing can stop the force of love.**

There is no way this energy will not be expressed. All these things will happen because I will never give up and I will hold my vision.

When I worked in photography I was really working by myself. I had jobs that took one or two days and some that would go for a week or two. On the longer jobs there was a feeling of teamwork, in fact, people would often refer to the group as a team. After spending a week or two with people, there was often a kind of bonding that would form, and over the years I established quite a few friendships. I was exposed to people who worried, but most of the people in the industry didn't have a chance to affect my life so much with their fears because I never really saw them much, and consequently even though I knew a lot of people I never got too involved personally.

When I got involved in Cell Tech, this changed. I see the same people a lot. They have become my friends, and I feel part of a family. As I travel around the country I constantly meet new people, and because the work I do in the seminars is intense and personal, I feel close and share a lot of feelings with many people in the community. There have been many periods of my life where I have worried and been almost paralyzed with fear, but I kept it to myself. I wouldn't even tell Nathalie, because I didn't want her to worry.

At the time, I wasn't aware that other people worried also. I would have moments of deep distrust of myself and my abilities, and wonder if I would be able to support my family. I have never been very organized in terms of financial records, and even though I was always good at making money, I was also good at spending it, so I always seemed to have debts. Sometimes, I would think there was no way out, and so I would lie awake at night feeling depressed and lonely, with no one I felt I could talk to. There would sometimes be periods where I would go a few weeks without a booking and wonder if my career was finished. Working for yourself takes away all the support systems. In a way, it is the price you pay for the freedom of not having a boss. Back during that time, I really felt like I worried alone, because I felt very disconnected from everyone, even Nathalie. There was no one to talk to, since basically everyone hid their fears. So when I lay awake at night, worrying, I didn't realize that it wasn't just my fear I felt, but that my thoughts were congealed with lots of others that belonged to other people.

Since I have grown in awareness, I realize that if I feel a fear or worry start to creep into my life, that it is not necessarily mine, but someone else's coming my way and scanning my thought process, so to speak, to see if there are any sister thoughts that the fear and worry can latch onto. When everyone's network was growing so fast, people felt connected, upbeat, positive and energized. But as soon as there was a slight shift in the growth curve, people started to worry and let this worry permeate their lives.

> **Now that my faith feels more secure, now that I feel plugged into the Divine energy, I don't get so plugged into the worry anymore.**

A few years ago knowing that I was 60-70 thousands dollars short on my taxes would have created nightmares. Now I kind of look at it, say OK, and just trust that something good is going to happen so I can take care of it. I know that every time up to now the universe has always taken care of me. I do know that feeling fear and worry do not serve me. I am going to focus on solutions and not problems. I am going to let the threat of the fear galvanize me into action. I can see in this debt an opportunity to go out and increase my value in the market place. There are millions of dollars floating around out there so I will put myself in situations where some of those millions will pass through my hands into the hands of the tax people. I share this with you because I want you to know that I am just like you. I worry, I have fears but I am not going to let the fears stop me–not even slow me down. I am going to go through the fears and worry because they don't serve me. And if I can do it, you can too. If I was to focus on the fear and the worry rather than bless it and move on, I would only attract more of it into my life. I don't want to just deny it either. I truly acknowledge it, for I trust there is a great gift in it for me. When I tap into the universal consciousness, I am tapping into a power much bigger than me. I can connect with all the empowered consciousness that has overcome every challenge that has ever existed. I know that faith and love is much better than some technique or strategy, because if I don't think that something is possible, there is no strategy that will allow me to accomplish it. Fear and worry is blocked love and blocked love translates to pain. Pain is not the truth, love is. Pain is what we go through on our way to love and truth.

If we are to build something, whether it is a downline, another business, a relationship or anything, we must believe in what we are building. When we are passionate and intense and totally loving what we are doing our belief is correspondingly strong. With strong belief, unshakable faith, positive attitude and a totally loving heart all focused in the moment, we are able to create because we are an extension of pure creative energy. As we all learn how to transform ourselves, we can collectively join together to transform the world. And this will happen as we walk in awareness.